IT HAPPENED
LIKE THIS

ADRIENNE LINDHOLM

IT HAPPENED LIKE THIS

a life in alaska

MOUNTAINEERS
BOOKS

MOUNTAINEERS BOOKS is the publishing division of The Mountaineers, an organization founded in 1906 and dedicated to the exploration, preservation, and enjoyment of outdoor and wilderness areas.

1001 SW Klickitat Way, Suite 201, Seattle, WA 98134
800-553-4453, www.mountaineersbooks.org

Printed in the United States of America
Distributed in the United Kingdom by Cordee, www.cordee.co.uk

21 20 19 18   1 2 3 4 5

Copyeditor: Chris Dodge
Cover and book design: Jen Grable

The views expressed in this book are solely the author's and do not necessarily represent the views of the National Park Service or other federal agencies.

Library of Congress Cataloging-in-Publication Data is on file

Mountaineers Books titles may be purchased for corporate, educational, or other promotional sales, and our authors are available for a wide range of events. For information on special discounts or booking an author, contact our customer service at 800-553-4453 or mbooks@mountaineersbooks.org.

♻ Printed on recycled paper

ISBN (paperback): 978-1-68051-134-5
ISBN (ebook): 978-1-68051-135-2

For my girls

CONTENTS

JUST ONE SUMMER

My luggage stacked on the curb at Philadelphia International Airport was its own declaration of independence. I was twenty-six, and although my parents didn't expect me to live within walking distance, they hadn't anticipated I'd want to move to the Arctic. I had no idea what a backcountry ranger did—especially in Denali National Park. We were just told to show up. So I'd tallied my savings and bought a plane ticket to Fairbanks, Alaska.

For several weeks my parents had asked over and over, "How long are you planning to stay? Is there a phone? What about bears?" I knew what they were really asking was, "Are you sure you want to go?"

On the drive to the airport Mom was still processing the details of my appointment. "It sure sounds rustic," she said, letting the words hang between us. And then, as we pulled up to the curb, "Maybe all those years you spent sleeping on the floor will pay off."

She was referring to the five years spanning part of elementary school and middle school during which I had refused to make my bed. As a consequence, my parents didn't allow me to sleep in the bed, so I slept in a sleeping bag on the floor beside it. Even though we lived in the urban East Coast, where camping wasn't part of most people's vocabulary, after a while no one in my family thought it was strange, and I can't remember how or why I ever returned to sleeping in a bed.

I turned to say good-bye. Dad pulled me into his chest. "I met some tough people up there," he said. Fifty years ago, barely a man, Bobby Lee had taken the only path that existed out of an impoverished community in North Carolina. He had enlisted in the US Army and been stationed in Alaska, where he worked as a cryptographer during the Korean War.

He gripped my shoulders. "You're going to do great, as always."

I felt the sting of tears, and I wondered how leaving for Alaska could feel like strength and sorrow at the same time.

In truth, I didn't feel so strong. I felt uneasy, but this wasn't because of the uncertain condition of my lodging or the many unknown details of a new job in a rugged and remote part of the country. The feeling, I see now, was guilt. My parents and younger brother were unwaveringly loving and supportive. Despite Dad's rigorous schedule as vice president of a paperboard packaging company, he showed up at every one of my soccer games. Mom and Dad drove me to gymnastics, lacrosse practices, and sports camps and endured two school plays each year. They helped me research colleges. They bought me a used car. But it wasn't enough to keep me on the East Coast. After high school, I had moved farther and farther away, first to Virginia and then to Colorado and Montana, even though I knew it made them sad. As much as I loved them, I simply couldn't ignore the restlessness welling inside me, the need to prove my strength to the world, to myself.

I lifted my backpack from the curb and slung a duffel bag over my shoulder. As I turned toward the sliding doors, Dad smeared a tear from his lip, and Mom waved, with her head cocked to the side. As usual, they were standing by, silently supporting my quest to find my own true north. *Onward*, I told myself, and then I turned away. I was headed to Fairbanks, where I didn't know a single person.

Though I carried meager belongings, my confidence was buoyed by a set of life skills I'd acquired in suburban Philadelphia, a stellar academic transcript from a private university in Virginia, my shiny new graduate degree in environmental studies, and a growing number of miles on my hiking boots.

A couple years of dabbling in environmental nonprofit organizations had inspired me to crusade for a world in which people cared more deeply about the fate of nature. I ached to contribute to this revolution. For just one summer I wanted to be part of something noble that would help preserve one of the wildest places on earth.

The engines revved. The jet charged down the runway and lifted off. I pressed my forehead to the window and watched the city recede. It was time to go to the mountains.

———

Mountains had discovered me as much as I had discovered them. I was eleven years old when I watched my mom spend winter nights kneeling over a huge map of the United States spread across our living room floor. She held a yellow highlighter as she paged through encyclopedia volumes and traced a route on the map.

"We're going to live out of the car for a month and sleep in a tent every night," she told my eight-year-old brother Scott and me.

In the kitchen I heard her explaining the trip to my dad: "I've always wanted to see the national parks. Are you sure you can't come?"

"Maureen, I'm afraid I can't take an entire month off work, but I'll join you toward the end. You pick the spot."

In late June she packed the Oldsmobile with our clothes, a cooler, a canvas tent and cotton sleeping bags, the coffee can stove I'd made in Brownies, and plastic plates and bowls. Scott and I crawled into the backseat, and we headed west toward I-70. In a couple hours we had left the traffic, shopping malls, and pavement behind. When we got to western Pennsylvania, my eyes were wide open. I had never seen that much open space before. Scott and I laughed at the cows.

Over the next two weeks we walked down into the damp, dripping, colorful Carlsbad Caverns, took pictures of bison and geysers at Yellowstone National Park, and hiked in the Grand Tetons.

When I walked to the rim of the Grand Canyon, I was unprepared for that level of grandeur. For a moment, I couldn't swallow. The red rock walls cascading down, down, down; so much space it made me a little dizzy; the smell of pine on the warm breeze.

It was the middle of summer and midday. It must have been over one hundred degrees. But we couldn't help ourselves. We started to walk down and then, after a mile or two, realized we would need to walk back up. I remember staggering into the shade and pressing my fingertips against the shaded rock wall for balance, sweat burning my eyes, cheeks flushed, and how wiping my cheek felt like wiping sandpaper because I was smearing salt across my face.

We made it back to the top, and over the course of that month, along the way, something shifted inside me, and I understood on some level that I'd been missing out.

But soon I was a teenager, and there were boys and parties, fitting in, and grueling academics, the East Coast pressuring me toward its own definition of success. I sort of forgot about mountains.

Until I met Holly at the University of Richmond. We became friends my freshman year, and our mutual love of riding bicycles and discovering tree-lined routes through the city bolstered our relationship. She was a year ahead of me and had long chestnut hair and emerald eyes. She spoke of the Rockies as a holy place, the West as a storehouse of possibilities. I remembered the Grand Canyon and believed her.

―――――――

It was almost the end of my junior year. Fed up with final exams, Holly and I had escaped to a coffee shop to write in our journals, but instead we found ourselves talking about beauty and dreams. She wrapped her fingers around a mug of hot tea, leaned across the table as if she was about to tell me a big secret, and said, "Beautiful things exist in greater quantities the farther west you travel."

I grinned, waiting for her to say more. She had encouraged me to take a religion class called "Goddess Traditions," a course that explored the sacred role of nature and women worldwide. Taking that class felt conspiratorial at our conservative Southern university and a little like betraying my beloved atheist father, but I was too intrigued by nature and by Holly not to take it.

"Look around," she whispered, "These people probably don't even *know* about the mountains."

I looked around. I couldn't tell what the coffee shop patrons knew about mountains or what wisdom the western landscapes supposedly held for us. I nodded in agreement anyway. I knew one thing for sure: we both wanted to try on a different landscape. I sensed something untamed in myself that needed to roam beyond the Eastern Seaboard. And if Holly thought there was a reason we should go west, then I was going to be the first to sign up to go with her.

School had been out only a few days when my mom dropped me off at Holly's house in Lancaster, Pennsylvania. I opened the door before the car came to a stop and jumped out before she could tell me to wait a minute. Holly and I were headed west.

The first night after Holly and I drove to Crested Butte, Colorado, we sat on a rooftop with our legs dangling over the edge, the little mountain town sparkling beneath our toes. The night was still and smelled of Ponderosa pine and sage. Looking up, stars spilled like sand across the blackboard night sky. I had never seen stars like that before, had never been in a place dark enough. Neither of us spoke for a long time.

Holly and I spent a week trying to find waitress and hostess jobs, but apparently there were a lot of people like us looking for that type of work. We settled for housekeeping positions at an upscale lodge on a golf course. Our supervisor, Louis, was our age, with black greasy hair, thick glasses, and an inclination to assert his authority. One day, Holly and I were in the bathroom in one of the suites. I was washing the sink, and Holly was hanging fresh towels when Louis walked in. "Have you cleaned the bathtub?" he snipped.

"I was just about to get to it," said Holly. She dropped to her knees and began washing the bathtub's faucet.

"See the back corner of the tub?" Louis directed. "You're not done until it's shining."

She grabbed a foul-smelling bottle with the word ENZYMES written on it in big black letters with magic marker. Louis stood over her as she scrubbed harder, not looking up.

Later in the day, cleaning another room, Holly found a G-string in the bedding and used condoms on the floor, then moved to the porch to wash windows and get some fresh air. She was clutching the ENZYMES bottle with one hand and scrubbing with the other, and a minute later I saw tears rolling down her cheek. I couldn't tell if she was laughing or crying, and it seemed reasonable she was doing both. I went out to join her.

"I turned down Andersen Consulting to do *this*," she said, holding up the bottle. "What the hell *is* this stuff anyway?"

We both started laughing, and we didn't stop until our bellies ached. I thought of the overachievers from our university who had resumes similar to Holly's: declaring straight A's and showing just the right combination of leadership, initiative, and involvement. They were back East having taken the high-paying jobs at the likes of Andersen, the top consulting firm in the country, which Holly had turned down to teach English in a remote village in southeastern Hungary, where she planned to go at the end of the summer. Her dream was to eventually write stories and books, but first she wanted something to write about. She misquoted Thoreau and told me, "How dare I sit down to write when I haven't stood up to live."

"Well," I told her, "we may be making five dollars an hour scrubbing toilets and pulling condoms from the carpet, but at least we're not wearing high heels and panty hose." I gave her a hug, and we stared across the golf course at rugged peaks cutting into the unfathomably blue sky. The sun reflected off patches of snow in high couloirs and beamed across our faces.

"God, it's gorgeous here," she sighed. Then she raised her hand for me to high five. "No price tag on *this* kind of beauty, sister."

At that moment, Louis walked through the door.

He shook his head. "I can't leave you two alone for a second. What do you think this is? You can't just take breaks when you feel like it. Get to work!"

We froze as his narrow eyes darted around the room, looking for something else that needed scrubbing. I wondered if our predicament would shake Holly's commitment to her dreams or her love affair with mountains. With her at the helm I felt dedicated to our quest, but I wasn't sure what I'd do if her motivation waned, so I rejoiced when I saw her scowl at Louis. She wasn't going to be defeated easily.

When our shift finally ended, we biked to the grocery store, where we bought a half gallon of rocky road ice cream and then opened it on the bench outside the store. At high altitude, the sun burned our scalps as we scooped ice cream into our mouths with our fingers. "I fucking hate Louis," I said.

"Those stupid glasses," she said, "like he's so smart or something."

We scooped ice cream until our fingers turned numb.

The next afternoon we decided to take our frustration with Louis into the mountains and let the mountain air sweep it away. We found a little trail off a narrow dirt road and followed it on foot up to a rocky overlook. We discovered caves up there, and we noticed wildflowers just starting to bloom. Infatuated, I inhaled deeply, feeling like the air was purifying my entire body. *This is the life I want*, I thought. These mountains were heaven on earth. How had I not realized that I could actually live in a place like this, that beautiful places aren't just sightseeing stops on a cross-country tour? It was hard to imagine returning to Richmond for my senior year, especially without Holly. I implored myself to remember, when I got back to school, what it felt like to live with all my senses, what it felt like to have a calm space inside my chest.

It was about eight o'clock that evening when the police officer called. I was alone at our apartment. "Is this Adrienne?" he asked. "Do you know Holly Payne?"

"Yes," I said slowly, struggling to understand why the police might be calling.

"She was in an accident," he said calmly.

"What?" I said, clutching the kitchen counter. My voice shook. "What happened? Where is she?"

"She was on the shoulder of the road and was hit by a car. We're taking her to the Gunnison Valley Hospital."

I arrived at the scene to see paramedics loading a stretcher into an ambulance. I couldn't tell if she was alive. Hands shaking and driving erratically, I followed the ambulance thirty miles south to Gunnison. From the waiting room I heard a blood-curdling scream, and I cried out to no one, "What the hell are they doing to her!" Then I thought, *Thank God she's alive.*

Finally, a doctor came out and told me that Holly had a broken femur and a shattered pelvis. "We have her femur in traction," he said. "She's awake but in pain. You can see her now if you like."

"Holly," I said, rushing to her bed. "How are you?" I wanted to gently hug some part of her body but was afraid to touch anything but her hand. I expected her to make a joke or some "they can't get me down" remark, but she just mumbled and stared at the ceiling with tears in her eyes, looking terrified and exhausted.

Later she told me that she had been on the side of the road giving two cyclists a flashlight so they wouldn't have to bike home in the dark, when a drunk driver had come by and hit them. Holly suffered the worst injuries of the three and had to have extensive surgery to pin her leg back together.

"There's a reason this happened, you know," she finally said. "I don't know what it is yet, but maybe—" Her voice trailed off.

After two weeks in the hospital, she was released to a wheelchair-accessible guesthouse where she would spend the rest of the summer. The doctors told her that it might be a year or more before she'd be able to walk again. Even after the accident, *especially* after the accident, there was no place she'd rather be than in the mountains. But now a quiet knowing existed between us—that she would carry a scar with her for the rest of her life, deeper than the foot-long one on her thigh that covered a titanium plate and a bunch of screws. A scar like one from a heart broken after a first love.

———

Without Holly, I hated Louis and the housekeeping job even more, but I was determined to stay in Crested Butte. Soon after the accident, I went to a tree-planting event and met a girl my age who had also recently moved to Crested Butte. The two of us decided to set out on a four-day backpacking trip in the Maroon Bells–Snowmass Wilderness, though neither of us had been backpacking before. I bought my first backpack and borrowed a tent and some other camping equipment. Our packs extended far behind us because we had strapped big puffy sleeping bags to them. Wildflowers were waist-high and covered the meadows in red, purple, yellow, and blue. We didn't know what any of them were called except columbine, Colorado's state flower. It took all day to crest Buckskin Pass, and when we did, we saw the jagged outline of the fourteen-thousand-foot Maroon Bell peaks shouldering up into the blue sky. Everywhere we looked was the most beautiful view we'd ever seen.

We had brought cans of soup for dinner but neglected to pack a can opener. We used rocks to pound metal tent stakes into the top of the cans and finally made enough holes to pour out the soup. Later I unrolled my inflatable sleeping mattress and didn't know I was supposed to inflate it. The ground was hard and cold, but in the morning I lied and said I'd slept fine. For breakfast we ate instant oatmeal in cold water because neither of us could get the stove to light. None of this mattered. Snowmass Lake glistened silver and blue. Each new series of alpine lakes we hiked to was a surprise. Lungs searing from the altitude, we trudged for a couple hours toward a high pass. I set my gaze on the top. As we got closer, I tingled with anticipation of what might appear on the other side. When we reached it, a row of peaks larger than any I'd ever seen swept toward the horizon, and wildflowers filled the valley below. I couldn't recall ever feeling so satisfied.

––––––––––

Heading to Alaska, I settled back into my airplane seat, closed my eyes, and smiled at the thought of that Colorado summer, because it was during that summer that I'd felt direction for the first time. It wasn't a sense of north or south. It was a feeling that my inner compass could, and would, find its own way. The destination hadn't been clear, but I'd had the vague sense that to discover my own truth, I should hold the magic of wild places close to my core. As soon as I graduated from college I'd moved to Boulder, Colorado, and for the next several years funded my outdoor lifestyle by working as a receptionist and secretary at an engineering firm, a laborer in the city's forestry division, and a salesperson at an outdoor equipment store. Outside of work, I'd sunk into mountain meadows, felt western waters run through me, and skipped through my days collecting encounters with beauty like a child plucking dandelion crowns. I'd learned lessons in scale and perspective, and the power of the mountains had dazzled me. I'd had no choice but to let them nudge me onto a new course. It was one that would lead me far from my childhood home, to a new home.

I had played in the mountains and chased adventures and boys in Colorado, Utah, and Montana, never staying anywhere long enough to fit in. I had learned how to mountain bike and begun competing in races. I had followed new friends up imposing peaks and learned how to navigate with a map and compass and how to travel lightly. I had embarked on solo excursions and long-distance hikes. I'd been afraid of getting lost, afraid of getting hurt, afraid of not making it. And sometimes I had gotten lost or hurt, and sometimes I had failed to do what I'd intended, but I had learned something and every day felt stronger and more competent.

What if the next place is more beautiful? I had thought. *What if it has greater challenges? What if the people are more intriguing?* So I had kept moving. Without the responsibilities of family, children, a career, or even a hint of a serious romantic relationship, I had been totally free to test myself in ways that most of my peers from Pennsylvania were unable to. I had wanted to form my own opinions without the constraints and feedback from family, bosses, or boyfriends that might make my choices less mine. Many people I knew back east, including my family, seemed happy there and enjoyed nature too, but there was something about so much development and busyness that didn't feel right to me. Maybe I couldn't handle the expectation of securing a high-paying career and owning a big house, but those things didn't feel as rewarding to me. *The farther I am from the East,* I'd thought, *the better chance I'll have of defining success for myself.*

Then someone had mentioned Alaska. "The biggest mountains of all," they'd said, and I knew I had to go.

As the plane winged north, I rifled through my spiral-bound notebook to review the page where I'd scribbled my approach to living. I tilted the notebook away from my seatmate so that she couldn't peek:

- Respect nature.
- Religion is neither practical nor useful. As Dad says, "Don't believe for a minute there's some god out there who's gonna save you." *Spirituality*, is that a New Age term for religion?
- Technology and development: evil, obviously. Fight development where it threatens nature.
- Children compromise a woman's ability to wring the nectar from life. I, for one, will not be having any.
- Killing, including hunting, is barbaric and wrong.
- Don't rely on anyone to take care of you. You don't need a husband.

Alaska will be a good place to live by these tenets, I thought.

The run-down hostel in Fairbanks where I spent my first night in Alaska fit perfectly into the way I thought my world should be ordered. This was a real cabin in Alaska, with log construction, creaky floorboards, and old traps and mining equipment tacked to the walls. *If Holly could see me now*, I thought, *she would totally approve.*

I was assigned to a room and found my way to an empty bunk. The room was cluttered with backpacks, shower sandals, drying laundry, and eight other people. *They must be true travelers*, I thought.

"I'm on my way to Denali," I told them with feigned confidence, which got a nod of approval, but I had nothing else to contribute, so I sat quietly on my bed and listened to tales of where they'd been and where they were headed. They spoke of towns and mountains and rivers I'd never heard of.

As I climbed into bed, I wrapped myself in my sleeping bag to stay warm. I waited for darkness to set in but it never did, so I put a shirt over my eyes to block the light of the midnight sun. Haunted by thoughts of what the summer might be like, I rolled from one side to the other most of the night.

The following morning, bleary-eyed and somewhat dazed, I took the shuttle down the Parks Highway to Denali National Park, where I'd gotten a job as a backcountry ranger through the Student Conservation Association. After spending six months thru-hiking the 2,159-mile Appalachian Trail and otherwise hiking and biking in the Rocky Mountains nearly every day since I'd graduated from college, I thought I had a fair amount of backcountry experience. So did the rest of the twentysomethings who had come from around the country to spend a summer in Alaska's premier national park, where Denali, the tallest mountain in North America, rises ghostly white to more than twenty thousand feet and enchants the sea of green tundra that surrounds it.

When our supervisor assigned us our first backcountry patrol, I found myself paired with Jeff, the only member of the backcountry staff who actually lived permanently in the area. The other rangers sat with their partners and excitedly ran their fingers over maps, speculating on what they might encounter and deciding what gear they would share and how many days of food to plan for. Jeff, meanwhile, seemed to roll his eyes as he looked over those in the group, most of whom were about half his age. As I walked toward him, he turned his back to put on his jacket. I paused beside a large wall map of the park and searched for the drainage we'd been assigned. When Jeff scooped up his belongings and headed for the door, I sheepishly intercepted him. "So, you know where we're going?"

"Been going there for decades," he said with a look that added "how about you?"

"Anything in particular I should bring?" I asked.

"Standard stuff," he said. "We'll take the camper bus tomorrow at ten. See you there." He turned and walked out the door.

I winced and stood there for a minute, hoping no one had witnessed my rejection. Quietly I gathered my things and slunk back to my cabin. *Maybe I never should have come here*, I thought. How could my supervisor have paired me with *him*? I threw my bag across the bed and sat down with a sick feeling in my stomach.

Although the weather was delightful the next day, my stomach was still in a knot as Jeff and I rode the bus into the park. Hours passed while I stared out the window and listened to other passengers' conversations. As the bus approached the rise in the road by the Stony Overlook, everyone on the bus gasped at the same time. People cut off their conversations and stared at Denali, that 20,310-foot massif looming giant and snowy out of the tundra foreground. Some people were moved to tears, and I quickly blinked to stifle my own emotion, embarrassed to show any sign of vulnerability to Jeff. The bus driver remained silent, knowing that when the simple act of viewing a mountain took his passengers' breath away, there was nothing he needed to say. *Whatever happens*, I thought, *this is the most amazing place I've ever been.*

Our patrol began on a trail that went for only a quarter mile before fading into alders and willows along the river bar. Feeling like I needed to prove my strength, I hiked faster than he could on the trail section, but as soon as we hit the brush I came to a near halt. I'd never hiked off-trail before. In Denali National Park, there is only one road in six million acres, and once you're off the road there's virtually nothing to interrupt the vast expanse of wilderness: no settlements, developments, or infrastructure that make it easy for people to get there and stay there. One of the things I hadn't considered when I applied for the backcountry ranger position was the fact that I'd never navigated through country without trails, bridges, signs, or campgrounds. I'd also never traveled through country with grizzly bears and wolves.

Jeff blazed ahead, thrashing through the alders and willows, wisely choosing a route through the thinnest branches and keeping us on course. I could barely keep up and had no idea how he knew where to go. I tried to look up out of the brush to get my bearings, but, when I did, I stumbled over branches and rocks. I powered through as fast as I could and tried not to lose sight of Jeff's back. There I was with all my experience and independence, hating the fact that right now I needed Jeff.

When we had to cross the river, Jeff simply trudged through it. Accustomed to dry Rocky Mountain hiking with few creek crossings, my instinct told me to sit down and take off my boots before wading across in order to keep my feet dry. But after seeing Jeff cross, I wasn't sure whether this was a test to see if I was dumb enough to get my feet wet—or whether it was a test to see how well I could ford a river. Jeff looked at me and then looked impatiently at his feet and sighed. *Forget wet feet*, I thought, *I can't let him leave me.* I stepped into the coldest water I'd ever felt, restrained a grimace as the icy water seeped through my hiking boots and socks, and felt my way across. I pretended it didn't hurt that much as I stepped out of the river with feet that were burning from cold.

Fortunately, I had enough sense after the first day to realize that I didn't know much about this country and that Jeff did. As much as I didn't want to admit it, I could probably learn something from him. So I began asking questions. How long have you lived here? What do you like most about the park? What's it like to see a wolverine? How do you know where the patrol cabin is?

At first his responses were a single word. Later they were one sentence. By the last day of our patrol we sat side by side on a grassy hillside above a wide river bar.

"You have to pay attention," he said.

He noticed my confusion. I knew I had to look out for wildlife and make sure no animal surprised me and got any of my food. The weeklong backcountry ranger training prior to our patrol had established this as the Golden Rule of Denali. It was the only way wild animals would stay wild and safe. I knew that already. "I'm scanning the river bar for bears," I told him.

"You might be looking at the river," he said, "but you have to look behind you too, so you can see the wolf coming down the hill. You have to be alert and look in all directions. All the time."

He wouldn't let me lounge back and take a nap in the sun. "There are animals all over the place that want your lunch, and I have to shoot them when some hiker lets them get food," he said, shaking his head.

"And besides," he told me, "these are animals people come from all over the world to see. Why you'd want to waste a nap over that—"

"People really do come a long way to see these animals, don't they?" I asked.

"No," he started. "I mean, yeah, they do, but—Look, you could go to a zoo and see every animal out here, right?"

I nodded.

"There are big mountains that are a lot easier to get to. These people are paying huge bucks, spending fifteen hours on an airplane, and then cramming into a shitty school bus for eight hours into the park." He paused, and said, "No, it's not just the wildlife."

I returned from that patrol hungry for more, anxious to understand what Jeff was talking about. What was it about this place that made it more than a glorified zoo or a postcard-perfect picture? I saw it in their eyes: Alaskans, like Jeff, who'd spent a lot of time outside looked like they were privy to some great secret. I wanted to know what that secret was. I wanted to fit in like Jeff did. My academic degrees and professional experience didn't amount to diddly as far as Jeff was concerned. They weren't going to help me unlock the secrets of the Alaskan wilderness. The only way to belong was to start racking up miles on the ground in the park and let the wilderness teach me. I anxiously awaited my next assignment.

It would be a little while. We earned our patrols only after a week or two working in the visitor center, talking with tourists and helping them plan their trips.

One evening an elderly couple with a Southern accent returned from a trip into the park and stopped at the visitor center to tell someone about it. The woman smiled at me and said, "It wasn't just seeing the bear. It was seeing that bear leading her cubs through the tussocks, rooting up ground squirrels, and those snowy mountains behind her. The light, it was early in the morning, and the sun was low so her fur was glowing and the yellow light reflected off the side of the mountain." She turned to her husband. "Was that something or what?"

Her husband leaned in and said thoughtfully, "You can imagine that bear doing that for the last thousand years. It's like getting to see where life came from, where we all came from."

"Where are you all from?" I asked.

"North Carolina."

"You came a long way," I said.

"There's not much left in the world like this," she said, contemplating. "We've wanted to come for a long time."

We backcountry rangers were proud of our jobs as protectors of one of America's wildest, most special places. We were thrilled to work there and contribute to something we saw as good and noble. We worked hard. We worked long hours. We were polite to every visitor, even when they were impolite to us. We answered all their questions the best we could. We lived together in small, cold cabins with no running water. After dinner, we drank cheap beer and played cards. During the night we peed in milk jugs. And over the course of that summer, those big wild spaces did something to my psyche that I hadn't expected—they made it impossible for me to leave.

I had planned to stay for just four months, but a year later I was still in Alaska, living near Anchorage in Eagle River and working as an outdoor recreation planner for Denali National Park. Maybe it was the wild animals, or maybe it was the clean air and water. It could have been experiencing the rivers and glaciers and canyons on such an immense scale that one summer wouldn't suffice to absorb so much beauty. But I don't think that was the main reason. I think what kept me here is what all those things add up to. I wonder if that's what Ranger Jeff was trying to tell me: what makes this place special is what those tangible things collectively represent. It's the sense of something whole and complete and free from human control.

In the Denali Wilderness I'd experienced a force much greater than myself. It seeped into my psyche and began to sculpt my inner landscape, and then I had no choice. I needed to stick around and see what would happen next.

INTO THE CURRENT

I went to the pound in Anchorage and adopted a mutt with mischievous eyes and a sweet disposition. His coat had streaks of orange and amber, the color of Alaska tundra in late summer and early fall. Kind of how it looked outside my living room window when I brought him home. I named him August for that reason.

After dinner I took August for a walk through the neighborhood. The willow leaves, fireweed, and cow parsnip had smoldered into yellows and reds, and that familiar smell of warm decay rose up around us as we walked into a cool, misty wind. Our route through the neighborhood took about forty-five minutes. It was rare to see a car, so August was free to nose through fireweed and torment ground squirrels. On the return, he faithfully kept pace a few strides ahead of me.

We slogged up the gravel switchbacks of the driveway, and suddenly a flash of movement directly in front of me broke my walking trance.

Not fifteen yards away, a grizzly bear was walking down the driveway. In a moment of panicked clumsiness I nearly tripped over myself. My sneaker skidded to a stop. The bear stopped at the same time.

I impulsively shuffled backward. "August, come!" I called in a panic. "Come, now!"

In as stern a voice as I could muster I snarled, "Go away, bear." At such close quarters I didn't want to shout at the bear lest this incite an aggressive response instead of the desired one.

The bear looked right at me as if assessing my request, but it did not go away. Instead it slacked its jaw and grunted in my direction. I willed myself to stop shuffling backward, thinking that staying put might help the bear resist the urge to chase the thing that was fleeing. The bear didn't charge. Instead it rose onto its hind legs and towered over us.

Face to face with the bear, I became cognizant of every part of my body. Standing at a forty-five-degree angle to it, I felt my leg muscles twitch, poised to dive to the ground if the bear advanced. I could almost feel my fingertips touching individual molecules of air. I heard my own breath exiting my mouth. The encounter was a sponge that sucked up every irrelevant thought. What remained was my heartbeat, the hot breath of bear, and the reminder that I didn't always get to dictate the outcome of my life.

Without hesitation my brave (and perhaps not so smart) little dog charged the bear. The bear dropped down on all fours, lunged in our direction, then pivoted and allowed August to chase it into the gully away from the house. I ran for the door.

I stood there scanning for August's tawny backside or the flair of his tail. I expected to hear a grunt or a yelp or the excruciating cry of a dog that had been maimed, but there was no sound. In a minute August bounded up the driveway, panting heavily, and jumped around my legs. I ushered him inside and squinted out the window. The bear was out of sight, likely feasting on plump autumn blueberries.

Out of breath, I walked upstairs. "Holy shit," I muttered in the tingling aftermath of the adrenaline surge. I let out a sigh and brought August a treat. Damn, we had been lucky. I should have been paying closer attention. I immediately thought of my parents; I couldn't wait to tell them about this, though I might need to fudge the distance a little. I didn't want them to lose too much sleep.

Though I'd only been in Alaska two years, I'd accumulated enough bear stories to understand that wildlife encounters are fairly common for most Alaskans, even those who rarely venture out of Anchorage. In a single weekend the preceding summer the *Anchorage Daily News* had reported on two dramatic human-wildlife encounters within the city limits. The first had involved a twenty-one-year old coming home to find a pile of bear scat on his living room floor. He had proceeded to rip a decorative sword from the wall and go room to room searching for the bear. The second story was about a moose that had sauntered through the automatic doors of the emergency room at Providence Hospital. The event was captured by a security camera, and on the internet the following day you could view a clip of the moose entering the hospital, looking around, and calmly walking out.

Shortly after my encounter with the grizzly, I went to a potluck, where a dozen friends and I sat on the floor, cradling plates of curry, and chatted. I told them about the bear in my driveway.

"Outrageous!" boomed Butch. "This place is *crazy*." He had a huge smile, as if he couldn't wait to run into a bruin himself.

"Out of all of us," said Brij in his British Indian accent, "I would say Butch has the highest probability of being attacked by a bear because he is always carrying bacon."

"That's right," said Butch, patting his stomach. "I'd be way tastier than you, my friend," he said, looking Brij's lean frame up and down.

Brij laughed. He worked for an oil company but refused to drive a car and was widely known as "that skinny Indian guy who rides a bicycle everywhere."

Becky and Corrina, the tiniest among us, scooted into the circle. With a sharp flicker of fun in her eyes, Corrina pointed her can of Pabst Blue Ribbon at me, "I remember when you said you'd never run alone in Alaska."

"Technically I was walking," I said. "And I should probably take that back." Which was true. When I moved to Anchorage after my backcountry ranger job, I was steeped in Denali bear safety mantras. I cringed at the memory of my telling Corrina's aunt and uncle—who had lived in Anchorage for thirty years—that they were risking their lives by going into the mountains alone.

"I'd *never* run alone," I'd said and regretted it even before they cocked their heads and gave me a look that said I had no idea what I was talking about.

"I don't think I had adventures with such inherent risk until I moved here," Becky said.

"I don't recall ever considering walking up my driveway to *be* an adventure," I said.

"Ah," Brij wagged his finger at us. "It is a thin line between desiring adventure and wanting to be safe."

Throughout the evening people shared stories of their own wildlife encounters: the fox that followed the hiking group for three days in the Arctic, the moose someone had almost crashed into while riding a mountain bike, the bear that had stuck its head into a tent.

These new friends of mine were also relatively new to Alaska. They were from everywhere—every corner of the United States and a handful of foreign countries—and they had varied interests. Butch had started a Pop-A-Lock franchise and was determined to work only enough to pay rent and buy bacon. Brij had come to Alaska on a work visa and made a living as a petroleum engineer. Matt worked for a public radio station and already knew more Alaskans than the rest of us combined. Jeff was a construction worker, a ballroom dancer, and could run a 10K faster than almost anyone in town. Shelley worked for an environmental nonprofit. Joe was a doctor. Becky had come to Alaska with the US Air Force but was trying to figure out how she could make the state a permanent home. Corrina worked nights at a home for troubled youth and waitressed at Moose's Tooth Pub and Pizzeria.

Later that night I asked everyone why they moved here.

"I wanted to see what it was like," said Shelley. "The scale, the mountains, the wilderness—" Her voice trailed off as if she couldn't quite pinpoint it.

"Because it's *Alaska*," Matt said, waving his arm toward the Chugach Mountains outside the window, and I got the impression that he, like me, couldn't fathom all that was contained in that word.

About five people said something along the lines of this: "For the outdoor—um, everything. You know?"

No one had a clear answer, and no one said "for a job" or "for my family."

I wondered how many, like me, had left loving families to chase a dream. Every week when I talked to my parents they were eager to hear stories and see pictures. Dad wanted to know what Fairbanks and Kenai were like and wondered whether I'd ever travel north to Point Barrow. He had been stationed in each of those towns, and he was fascinated by how much Alaska had changed in fifty years. I encouraged him to visit, to see for himself, and he would—more than once. And with each visit my parents would seem newly relieved. "Your friends are so—positive," Mom would remark. "You really do look out for one another."

As the potluck wound down, Becky and I made plans to hike the next day and we all shared long, tight hugs. It was getting harder to feel the same ease with my friends in the Lower 48. Many were dedicated to advancing careers, and some were having children. All of them were living far from the wilderness that I was experiencing here. When I told them about hearing a wolf howl or how we got around a crevasse on a climb in the Chugach, they could only say "wow" and "huh." And as for me, I had no context for "married with children," and I wasn't even sure what questions to ask. I remembered in college feeling like I could confide only in Holly about my desire to live close to nature. My peers thought I was crazy for not wanting to get married, have kids, or own a television. Did I fit in any better here in Alaska? I wasn't sure yet, but more and more it seemed like the people who understood me the best were some of the people in this room.

Yet I still felt adrift, caught in the current between the shore of my old life and the opposite bank where I wanted to land but wasn't sure I truly belonged. The other day I had gone to REI and couldn't find water purification tablets. Instead of asking for help, I wandered the aisles for ten minutes until I found them. And another day I had been shopping for skis, and when the salesperson asked if I knew the different types of bindings, I pretended that I did. Why did I think I wasn't cool enough, or Alaskan enough, if I hadn't memorized the layout of the outdoor equipment store? I figured real Alaskans knew ski bindings just as they knew where to backcountry ski in any type of snow. They could subsist off the land. They didn't have to ask questions about bush planes and aluminum skiffs. Among them, I felt like an outsider. I had thought making good grades in school was all I needed to do. How could I ever have thought I would one day need to know how to use an avalanche beacon?

I dodged humiliation by relying on my friends. Jeff could fix anything. If you locked your keys in your car, Butch could help you out, day or night. Joe would save you a trip to the medical clinic. Brij produced detailed graphs and spreadsheets of our biking and hiking times and elevation profiles. He was also meticulous about research and could tell you about any piece of outdoor gear you were considering buying. Corrina showed up at potlucks with Moose's Tooth pizza. Becky took an avalanche course and offered to teach the rest of us.

What did I have to offer? Through my job I had opportunities to take shotgun training and classes in ATV driving, motorboat operation, wilderness first aid, and bear safety. I shared what I learned, and my job gave me a handhold on the cliff of self-doubt.

On our hike the next day, Becky and I climbed up into the mountains in Chugach State Park with August running along beside us. Every few steps we reached down to snap wild blueberries from their stems, popping them into our mouths. I told her that the National Park Service in Alaska was responsible for protecting a third of the country's wilderness areas. "We make it possible to have the type of adventures we all came here for."

As the words came out of my mouth I knew it was absurd to claim credit for preserving the wildlife and wilderness that is the heart of Alaska. I had an entry-level position on the Denali National Park team responsible for writing management plans. In addition to doing research for the managers, my job included data entry, filing, and taking care of other people's travel arrangements. The credit wasn't mine to take, but I couldn't help myself—like a dirt-poor girl trying on an Oscar de la Renta dress, I just wanted to see what it felt like.

Becky pulled herself onto a boulder on a ridge. "Did I tell you I always wanted to be a park ranger? Even as a young girl on the farm in Illinois."

I looked up at her. "You would be amazing. I could ask around at work and see if anyone's hiring."

"Maybe someday," she said, looking ahead along the ridge. "That could be cool."

I told her about some of the people I worked with—the permanent employees, not the transient ones. Many of them had been in Alaska during the 1970s when the law that established nearly all of the state's national parks was being debated. One of them, Page Spencer, would later become my supervisor. Page grew up on a homestead on the Kenai Peninsula where she and her brothers and sister cut and split and hauled firewood, brought water up from a creek when the well froze, had a giant garden, raised chickens and ducks, hunted moose, and picked berries. Her father became the supervisor of all the US Fish and Wildlife Service refuges in Alaska, and in time they named the wilderness unit around the Swanson River Canoe System for him. Her sister and brother skied in the Olympics. I marveled at how Page sewed her own fur parkas, flew her own airplane, filleted salmon, and made blueberry jam. While I couldn't imagine hunting and fishing, I could tell by the nostalgic look she got when she spoke about subsisting off the land and observing nature that those experiences were powerful and connecting for her. When the weather was perfect, she implored me to leave the office and play in the mountains. With a sparkly smile she said, "You *must* practice for retirement."

Becky listened intently. "Page sounds incredible."

"Yeah, she's the real deal."

"Why do you think the first question people ask is how long you've lived here?" Becky asked.

"Do you think it's like a test?" I offered. "That you have to earn your status by putting in time? Or what if the number of years is a proxy for competence? Maybe it's a way to gauge how comfortably a person is able to wear their Alaska identity."

I climbed up on the boulder to join Becky. After a minute Becky asked, "Do you feel judged when someone asks you that?"

"Sometimes—like until I rack up a certain number of years, my opinion doesn't count as much. But with people like Page, there's no judgment at all, only encouragement to love what's here."

"Maybe that's all it is," said Becky. "I mean, we already love Alaska. Maybe we'll feel like we belong once we feel more comfortable with all the different types of experiences we can have here."

I petted the top of August's head and considered that. I'd traveled to almost every state and had bicycled and backpacked in New Zealand, Japan, India, Europe, and several countries in South and Central America. This place—with wilderness on a scale unmatched in the rest of the country, the unassuming way Alaskan culture challenged mainstream norms, and a community of inspiring people—was different. I liked it here more than I'd liked any other place. The problem with traveling, I realized then, is that you never really belong.

We sat for a minute without speaking. A pika chirped behind a jagged fin of rock. I traced a trickle of water down the mountainside, out of the park, through town, to the delta that emptied into the ocean. The land and waters that surrounded us were wild and unhindered. They mirrored the freedom that I wanted for myself. I reflected on all that I'd loved about that past week: sharing dreams with friends with no fear of being judged; climbing mountains with no one else on them; the grizzly bear in my driveway, eating wild berries. It felt like the mountains and the bear and the red-yellow August tundra, all of it, had begun to filter into my bones.

That evening Becky and I piled on Butch's couch and talked about adventure racing, endurance contests that include a variety of self-propelled modes of travel through the wilderness. Becky had recently returned from New Zealand where she'd raced in the Eco-Challenge as a member of Team US Air Force. Butch, on the lookout for new ways to suffer, queried her about the course (navigating scree-covered mountains, crevassed glaciers, and wild rivers on foot, horseback, bike, and raft), what she ate (instant mashed potatoes and jerky in a Ziploc bag warmed in her sports bra as she hiked), and what type of gear she brought.

"Meeting the gear requirements and trying to go as lightweight as possible was interesting," she said. "We used nylons as a lightweight thermal layer, and for our medical kit I trimmed the edges off all of the pill packets to save weight."

"Skimping on warm layers and first aid," Butch bantered. "What could go wrong?"

We laughed as he continued, "So, overall, how much sleep are we talking about?"

"My team slept about nine hours total over six days."

"Badass," Butch concluded. "We oughta train for something together. If we train in Alaska, you know, nothing can be harder than that."

As Becky and Butch searched the internet for a long-distance race to enter, I looked out the window at the yellow cottonwood leaves on the sidewalk and then lifted my gaze across town and up into the mountains. I picked out the rocky ridge that Becky and I had teetered along that afternoon. Being free was more complicated than I'd thought. I needed to keep my job in order to pay the bills. My reliance on my friends seemed to go against my commitment to self-sufficiency, and my growing attachment to Alaska itself seemed to be at odds with being unencumbered. But I wanted to belong, which would entail the emotional investment of caring.

WHEN YOU GO INTO THE COUNTRY

My friend Shelley and I showed up on time at the little hangar near the gravel airstrip in Coldfoot, but the small plane that would carry us and our backcountry gear into the Arctic National Wildlife Refuge was slightly behind schedule. Maybe the pilot had decided to have a leisurely breakfast.

I was standing patiently in the air taxi office when an old man with a weathered face and oil-stained coveralls came through the door. Maybe he was waiting for the plane too. Maybe he was just looking for conversation. One thing was for certain: he knew with a glance that we weren't from here.

"When you go into the country," he told us, "you have only your-self to rely on."

We nodded respectfully.

"It ain't Colorado out there," he continued and waved his arm away from the airstrip. "Sure ain't no Lower 48 excuse for mountains."

I smiled politely, thinking, *I know that.* At least he didn't make a joke about being from Anchorage, how it's only an hour from Alaska or some bullshit like that. Part of me felt an unbridgeable cultural divide between rural Alaska and the city. It was hard to convey to peo-ple living off the road system or in small villages why I liked living in Anchorage and that, to me, a community of three hundred thousand people spread over a municipality the size of Delaware was a small town.

I looked out the window and saw two teenage boys zoom by on ATVs, a cloud of dust in their wake. A woman behind the desk laughed into the phone, called someone darling, and told them to check back with her in an hour. She popped open a can of Diet Coke. My eyes shifted around the room and landed on a pot of coffee beside a grease-stained sofa. I poured coffee into a Styrofoam cup and took a seat beside Shelley. After the sixteen-hour drive from Anchorage to Coldfoot, and camping en route along the side of the road, a little coffee felt necessary.

When I saw the plane, it looked smaller than I thought it should. We knelt down at our pile of gear to recheck all of it.

"You packed the tent, right?" said Shelley.

I nodded. "Do you think three canisters of fuel will be enough? I have six dinners and you have six dinners, right?"

Shelley unzipped the outer pocket of her backpack and reached inside. "You grabbed those extra two lighters?"

Once we left, there would be no going back.

The pilot showed up wearing a flannel shirt and a faded baseball cap. It looked as though he hadn't shaved in a week. He told us to carry the gear to the scale, where he weighed it, and then to the plane, where he loaded it behind the seat. He fueled up while we stood beside the hangar with our hands in our pockets.

"Want the front seat?" Shelley offered, as if it was an honor to sit beside the pilot.

"No, you should take it," I said. I knew that we both wanted the backseat so that we would feel less obligated to make conversation and because it would be easier there to look out both sides of the plane. I climbed in the back and strapped in. The plane lifted, and I saw that Coldfoot was a pinprick of development on a quilt of undeveloped land. The pilot talked about the musk oxen he had seen on his preceding flight and where the caribou had been last week. I wondered if he would comment on our itinerary or ask about our route, but he didn't.

Coldfoot vanished quickly, and, as soon as it did, a feeling came over me that I hadn't felt in a while. It was the feeling of something about to happen. A feeling as sure as the raw Arctic air sweeping over my skin, whispering that soon it would be my turn to show up for my life. No one else was responsible now.

The expanse of the Brooks Range rose into view as we flew east over the Arctic National Wildlife Refuge toward the headwaters of the Kongakut River. This trip was going to be just what I needed. Now that I'd achieved permanent status with the National Park Service, I was putting in long hours on the backcountry management plan for Denali National Park. The debates around snowmobile use in the park, commercial services, wolf protection, and mountaineering on Denali were contentious. I considered the park to be a sanctuary for wildlife, and I was losing sleep knowing that the park service was allowing a level of motorized use of the park that might be harming resident animals. Predators seemed especially vulnerable. I had begun to consider wolves and bears our brothers and sisters in the global community of life, and it saddened me to learn about the ways they were being legally hunted and trapped both within and outside national parks in Alaska. With every foot of elevation we gained in the plane, it seemed that the Arctic Refuge was going to be exactly what I needed to refresh my perspective.

The flight took about two hours. During that time we spotted no other people. I watched sunlit tundra unfold to the horizon and a quiet river wind into a little gorge and then reemerge. I saw gentle green and gravelly mountain ridges—and the dark back of a bear. The sides of the foothills looked raked by the fingernails of a giant, and it took me a moment to realize they were caribou trails streaking across the refuge. I tried but couldn't quite imagine how many caribou it must have taken to make all those lines. The two hours passed quickly. Our plane circled a gravel bar, and the pilot made sure there weren't any rogue sticks or big rocks or unexpected divots that could damage it. I held on and held my breath as the little aircraft trembled for a moment above the land and finally touched down.

Disembarking felt like it should take more time. I was compelled to ask the pilot if he wanted to stay for a cup of tea. But pilots are usually in a hurry. "Enjoy yourselves," he said. Then he spun the plane around, and for a second I felt the urge to yell, "Wait! I think I forgot something really important!" But there was nothing important I'd forgotten, only how to feel comfortable with myself in a quiet space with the few things Shelley and I had brought with us.

The plane took off and was out of sight and sound within a couple of minutes, leaving us with a large landscape to meet and get to know as we made our way to the Beaufort Sea. Shelley stared at the hollow space where the engine buzz had just been. In that intense quiet, I cautiously looked around. There were enormous mountains and a turquoise river and a sky that might swallow me.

The more I saw of Alaska's backcountry, the more I felt like an Alaskan, but the weather, the light, and the topography was different every time I traveled, so that each arrival felt a little jolting. Such is the beauty and consequence of air travel here.

"Where *are* we?" I squealed to Shelley.

Shelley burst out, "I can't believe we're finally here! This is amazing!"

"And it's all ours!" I jumped around for a minute and started running in place, and then I suddenly stopped. It was as if our voices didn't belong there, as if spoken syllables would tear the fabric of wind and rippling water and birds so exquisitely stitched together.

I stilled myself and whispered to Shelley, "What should we do now?" I glanced around for bears.

I knew it would take a night or two falling asleep to the hum of the river and waking up in the tent before I would feel like I belonged to that place. By the following day Shelley and I had established our routine, fetching water in the morning, eating cereal while dressed in puffy jackets, jamming sleeping bags into stuff sacks, and packing up the tent. Shelley splayed the map on the ground. "Do you think the ridge we want to get to is this one?" She pointed to a line on the map.

"It looks like there's a pass to the east. Want to see if it goes?"

We followed a creek, and after a while we stopped pointing out the bear, wolf, and caribou tracks. We climbed up a steep rise, and as we approached the top I saw a dash of brown.

"Shhh!" I put my arm out to stop Shelley. We crouched down. Shelley mouthed, "What?"

I shook my head and whispered, "Smaller than a bear."

We waited without moving. Soon it appeared, skittering around the ridge—the elusive wolverine. We watched it claw the earth and bound over the tundra. After a few minutes we lost sight of it and stood up to scan the mountainside. Shelley gave me an incredulous look and grabbed my arm. "Thank you for inviting me on this trip!"

On top I saw a rock fin that we would have to negotiate to stay on our route, and I worried that we wouldn't find a way to get past it. On closer inspection Shelley spotted a way to sneak behind it. "Everything goes here," she remarked casually. We ditched our backpacks behind a rock out of the wind, sat down, and let the sun warm our faces.

It was beginning: that feeling like my eyes were becoming the sun, my hair the wind, my fingernails the gritty riverbank, my feet the tundra. It was like an ancient part of me was remembering how to do this—how to survive out here and also how to open up and let it in. I listened to the breeze rustle tiny leaves. I thought I could detect the musky scent of wolverine.

During the night, rain bucketed down on our tent. In the morning the air was fresh and sweet, and I warmed my fingers on a hot cup of tea. We sat beside the stove watching the river. From the silence, a note of music rose and traveled across the valley floor: the haunting howl of a wolf. I looked behind Shelley, hoping. I stood on tiptoes. *To see one*, I thought, *would be all that I'd need to call this trip extraordinary.*

On the fourth day, I could hardly recall Anchorage. I couldn't fathom my office or email. I could barely remember what traffic sounded like or what my daily obligations were back in the city. Wolves had become the ordinary thing to think about. It was only a week ago that I was worried about preparing for a meeting at work. On the way home that day I had been stuck in traffic and anxious about a line at the post office. How did the refuge erase all of that?

I inhaled deeply, taking in purifying air and something else too, something even less tangible. An energy that is hard to describe seeped into every neglected part of my body and expanded into interstices between all my cells. It created a sensation of openness inside my mind and heart. I became aware that with each breath, I gained a more expansive perspective on my life. Anything seemed possible.

"Do you think you'll keep working for the Park Service?" asked Shelley as we wiggled into our sleeping bags that night.

I said that I thought I would—that I didn't enjoy being in an office but that I loved being part of decisions affecting the park. "I'm not sure, though, if I've really found my people there," I admitted. "Sometimes it seems like they're willing to compromise too much, like they're afraid to say no to anyone, even to people who want to do things that degrade the wilderness."

"Have you thought about working for an environmental group?"

"I worked for one for a few months, but I didn't think it was a good fit either. I couldn't take a hard line on all the issues. I'm not sure where I fit in, but if I hear one more person call a wolf a 'resource' I think I might hurt someone."

Shelley adjusted the ball of clothes she was using as a pillow. "What would an ideal work situation look like?"

"I tell you what it would look like—working from home and taking several months off every year to travel and enjoy Alaska."

We contemplated a future constructed exactly how we wanted it to be.

"Do you think you'll stay in Alaska?" I asked.

"To tell you the truth, these trips and our friends are amazing, but I haven't found a job that's right for me. Maybe I should go back to school. And you know, I miss being close to my family in Seattle. We'll see. How do your parents feel about you wanting to stay here?"

I rolled onto my back and pinched a mosquito against the tent wall. "I think they've accepted that we're all going to have to travel a lot to see each other." I wondered what they were doing that week. I knew Mom would be busy with her environmental group and local politics, but since Dad had retired he hadn't found anything that delighted him as much as being with my brother and me. I wished I had made more of an effort to talk with them.

"Hey, Shell, have you ever made a list of goals for the year?" I asked.

We talked about everything we would put on that list: calling our parents more often, researching options for going back to school, dedicating time each week to practice art, taking a ballet class, entering a mountain bike race, organizing a community talent show, volunteering to do trail work.

"To be our best selves," I said, "maybe the greatest thing we can do is cultivate the sense of openness that we feel out here." I began to recall with shame how I'd judged some of my Lower 48 friends for taking corporate jobs and allowing themselves to be tied down with kids so early in life. I had been hard on myself too. I questioned my adamant belief that it was a sign of strength to depend only on myself. What would it feel like to be more honest with myself, to really listen? Instead of doing what I thought I *should* be doing to appear strong, what if I chose a path that included self-care and honest reflection? I remembered meeting Page and observing how she confidently aligned her life with her values, and I recalled how I'd dismissed that as lucky. But after long slow days in the wilderness with Shelley, I started to think a balanced life *was* possible.

Before I fell asleep I began to catalog other things I felt adamant about. The first thing that came to mind was hunting. I remembered the look of disdain in my mom's eyes when her brother moved to Idaho and went hunting every chance he got. "Poor animals," she said. "Just awful." And I agreed. When I thought of hunting, I thought of pick-up trucks loaded with beer and ammunition, camo-clad men driving dirt roads looking for something to shoot at, maybe only to get the antlers. Dad shook his head too: "No sport in it at all."

Over the last few months, though, I'd gotten a chance to talk with locals from rural Alaskan communities, and I had to admit the way they hunted moose and caribou seemed different from every preconceived notion I'd had about hunting. I fell asleep feeling the world was not as black and white as I'd thought.

As the days passed, Shelley and I covered miles and closed in on the coastal plain of the Arctic Refuge. For a wilderness lover like myself this was sacred ground, the nation's symbolic battlefield of oil development versus wilderness, the fabled calving grounds of the Porcupine

Caribou Herd. As we descended a tundra slope above the plain we were engulfed by thick mist and decided to stop and make camp. The night was cold, and it rained hard. The corner of the tent leaked onto the foot of my sleeping bag. I shivered in the morning, had to work hard to warm my toes, and carefully plotted how to change my clothes without letting heat escape. I anticipated the flavor of almonds and dried mangos I would eat for breakfast.

Seeing the sky clear after a night of rain made me happier than I'd felt in a long time. Watching a golden eagle dive for a fish while we ate breakfast made me think that I ought to thank someone—it was such a fantastic gift. Later, running down the mountain made me feel like a kid, yelping and leaping and not worrying about anything. I saw what it meant to live in the present, to live for at least a day using all of my senses, to feel connected to something greater. All the things that seemed to matter at home, all the things by which I allowed myself to be defined—how well I did at work, how quickly I could climb a mountain, how well I fit in among my friends and Alaskan community—did not seem like the most important things anymore.

After nearly two weeks of backpacking and boating with Shelley, it had become difficult to talk about my job or my to-do list at home. They seemed so irrelevant. I was not my job, after all, nor was I my athletic ability or my imperfect body. I was not the accolades I'd received at work, and I was not the rejection I'd felt when the mountain runner guy that I liked started dating someone else. That wild place, the Arctic National Wildlife Refuge, showed me this, and I suppose that's why I had come. I relished this fresh perspective until the day before we were scheduled to meet the pilot who would fly us back to civilization.

By then my dwindling bag of trail mix was mostly peanuts. Otherwise we had one emergency dinner of pasta, a few dried banana chips gone soggy, and an energy bar. My two shirts stank and my down jacket was damp from the rain. My socks and shoes were permanently saturated. My hair was greasy and matted to my forehead.

Maybe I wouldn't mind a nice dinner out. Maybe a hot shower would feel good. I knew once those thoughts started, the trip would be over. But lousy weather could not be kept at bay. The plane might not be able to fly. The pilot might not come for another day or two or three.

We waited.

Our pile of gear was a bit smaller because our food was nearly gone. Shelley made a thermos of tea and sat on her pile of gear.

"What's the longest you've waited?" she asked.

"Three days, when we were fogged in on the coast."

I searched the sky. "Is that it?" I said, thinking I might have heard a far-off plane engine.

Shelley squinted, shook her head, and returned to where she'd left off in the book she was reading.

Some of the anxiety that I'd let go of began to creep back in. I beseeched myself to hold the feeling of spaciousness, but my mind was a trickster bent on convincing me of the importance of the work that had piled up in my office while I was gone, the looming social engagements, the car payment that was overdue. I sat beside Shelley and toggled between the wild and encumbered versions of myself.

After an hour of silence, Shelley perked up. "Do you hear that? Is that it?"

I strained but couldn't hear anything. It was nothing again. I wondered how long it would be. I wondered if we should pitch the tent. Near the end of the day I *begged* the plane to come. It was all I thought about.

"Ah!" I yelled finally. "That's it!" We both heard the engine. We scanned the sky. The plane angled in and touched down. Knowing that the adventure was now over, I felt sad for an instant. I glanced around one last time.

The pilot hopped out to load our backpacks, and I struggled to think of something to say. "Oh, thanks," I mumbled as I dragged my gear to the plane. It was just so weird that someone had dropped out of the sky into our realm.

I waited for him to strap our packs down and tried to reconcile my conflicting desires to stay and leave. Thriving in the wild had transformed me. I had become a new version of myself and had shed, however slightly and temporarily, the burden of modern convenience and the burden of my critical thoughts.

Lured by the promise of a shower and good food, I stepped toward the plane. Shelley gave the pilot her bright smile and climbed in the front seat. We easily lifted into the sky. Behind her, I smiled as she bantered with him the entire way home.

WOLVES

Becky thought she saw something move on the riverbank, so I wedged the paddle against the interior side of the canoe and groped in the bag on my lap for binoculars. Holding them to my eyes, I steadily scanned the willows along the Noatak River. The canoe drifted sideways until I felt Becky straighten it.

After a minute I glanced back at her and shrugged. "Don't see anything."

I couldn't help doing a double take. Seeing Becky in a National Park Service jacket made me smile. Being out here on a work trip with her felt like a pretty spectacular streak of good fortune.

Hearing the buzz of an approaching motor, I spun back around and palmed my canoe paddle. We edged toward the shallow side of the river in order to give the motorboat the deeper channel.

As the planning team at Denali National Park gained more experience resolving management challenges that were unique to Alaska, some of us were farmed out to help at other Alaska parks, particularly those with small staffs. In addition to continuing to work on backcountry management at Denali, I had begun assisting the Western Arctic National Parklands with resolving conflicts around subsistence and sport hunting. When I was asked to investigate the site of a potential new subsistence cabin in Noatak National Preserve, no park staff members were available to join me, so I had signed up Becky as a Park Service volunteer.

As we floated down the Noatak River in our collapsible canoe, we waved at motorboats full of local people presumably heading upriver to fish, hunt, or visit friends and relatives. Paddling a canoe in my brightly colored dry suit, I felt like a very different type of park user than the locals dressed in hooded sweatshirts motoring upriver in aluminum skiffs. Usually when I'm on a wilderness trip, if I see anyone at all it is others doing something similar to what I'm doing. Here our mission was different from that of the local subsistence hunter. Becky and I paddled past a hunting camp and waved. They stared back, and then one man took a couple steps toward the river. "You see caribou?"

"No, we haven't seen any."

The man stared at us as we floated past his camp.

"Good luck," I added.

The encounter felt awkward and interesting at the same time. Interesting because of the contrast of paddling through "wilderness"— even "our wilderness"—while indigenous people continued to use their homeland in a way that mirrored how their ancestors had used it for thousands of years.

But, of course, people don't use the land exactly as they did in the past. Times have changed, here as anywhere else. People now use snowmobiles (called "snowmachines" in Alaska) instead of dog teams, for example, and subsistence economy has been replaced by hunting and fishing blended with a wage economy. Before the trip Becky and I had both read Seth Kantner's *Shopping for Porcupine*, in which Kantner describes in exquisite detail how people used to live in Alaska's Western Arctic and how the old ways were the only way just a couple of generations ago. In a handful of decades so much has changed. Becky and I found it to be an inspiring account and testament to the closing of a chapter on the old way of doing things. I'd underlined a passage that now felt relevant as we floated by the hunting camp: "The dying of subsistence as a lifestyle doesn't negate the importance of wild food from the land, for many of us essential to feeling and being alive. The gathering of wild food has changed but still provides nourishment to our spirits too, something that doesn't seem to be coming off those airplanes. . . . We are living in the twilight of the frontier, in the headlights of America."

I told Becky I felt like we were in the front seat of that figurative car in Seth's book, peering into the space illumined by its headlights.

"It's pretty cool to be part of a landscape that's valued for so many reasons," said Becky.

On trips to Kotzebue, the hub of the Northwest Arctic, I was intrigued by how local people saw themselves in relation to the land and how their values for wild country differed from my own. Unlike most of the rest of the world, where islands of nature are engulfed by modern civilization, Arctic communities are like little islands in a sea of wild country.

Earlier that year I'd had an opportunity to help coordinate a radio program that asked the question "What does wilderness mean to you?" to people in Alaska living closest to it. The host had interviewed three lifelong residents and local leaders of Kotzebue. One of the men interviewed said, "It would be difficult to find anyone in the region who actually knew there were federally designated wilderness areas or who could point out where wilderness areas are on the map or on the ground."

However, they also concurred that the value of Northwest Alaska wilderness lands is their ability to provide food and meet other subsistence needs. People continue to hunt seals, walrus, caribou, moose, ducks, geese, and myriad other animals, and the wilderness designation protects them and their habitats so that traditional ways of life can continue. "Wilderness areas exist to ensure a way of life lives on in which man is part of the natural world," one elder said.

Before coming to Alaska, I'd never considered hunting animals a legitimate use of wilderness, but when the elders talked about the respect they had for the animals and how they considered themselves part of nature, not separate from it, and how humans and the land had evolved together for thousands of years, it made me reconsider.

As I listened to the interview progress, I was surprised to hear these leaders extolling federal lands, considering the role the US government played in changing their culture. Inupiat culture, like most indigenous cultures in the world, was decimated as Christian missionaries, traders, and settlers moved in during the late 1800s and early 1900s. I had recently read the memoir of Kotzebue native and former Alaska state legislator William Hensley, and his words about all that the Inupiat lost were still fresh in my mind. "My family and I were supposed to learn a new language, adopt profoundly different notions of private property; we were supposed to adjust our communal society to one based on capitalism, self-interest, and individual choice." When Hensley and other leaders took inventory of all that was lost, they affirmed that to restore Inupiat culture and identity, the most important connections to strengthen would be those among family and to the land.

During the years leading up to the Alaska Native Claims Settlement Act of 1971, Hensley and many others fought to secure traditional lands for the Inupiat people and for Native people across Alaska, and, in the end, Alaska Natives acquired title to forty-four million acres of land.

I rested my canoe paddle in the boat, and we let the gentle current carry us downstream. "Managing public lands is more complicated than I'd ever imagined," I told Becky. "Particularly because ANILCA tried to satisfy everyone."

"Alaska National Interest Lands Conservation Act, right?" she said.

"That's right." In 1980 Congress passed ANILCA, dedicating more than one hundred million acres in Alaska to conservation. "It's complicated in part because it allowed local people to continue to live off the land."

The authors of the legislation also acknowledged that people all over Alaska were using numerous modes of transportation to travel between homes and villages and to hunt, fish, trap, and collect berries and other edibles. In order to accommodate traditional activities and transportation needs, Congress included unprecedented special provisions for motorized use of Alaska's wilderness.

"So *that's* why we have people doing subsistence and driving motorboats in the parks and wilderness areas here but not in the Lower 48!" Becky said.

"Exactly."

As we paddled on, I felt humbled knowing that some people not only equate this land with freedom and challenge, as I do, but with food, survival, and indelible cultural associations.

A week after that paddle trip with Becky, I learned that more than sixty wolves had been shot dead during the state's latest round-up, near Yukon–Charley Rivers National Preserve, in the name of decreasing the number of predators so hunters have more abundant moose, caribou, and sheep to hunt. It left me wringing my hands and tossing in bed at night. Initially, I'd thought predator control was something of the past, a bloody part of our nation's history that we'd learned from and gotten over. After decades of extirpation, Lower 48 states had begun reintroducing wolves and grizzly bears. While reintroductions remained very controversial, it seemed like a growing majority had recognized the value of predators to ecosystems and economies. Besides, I thought, these are our national parks. Didn't the National Park Service have control over what happens there?

The situation, like so many in Alaska, was more complicated than I first thought. The State of Alaska has jurisdiction over wildlife throughout the state, but the federal government cannot allow wildlife management practices that conflict with the purposes of federal land, a fact the state had begun to challenge. This power struggle between the state and federal government received widespread coverage in state news.

A coworker, Linda, was intrigued by the controversy. "Does the ethical argument against predator control ever factor into it?" she asked.

"I'm guessing the ethical argument would have to come from the public and that the National Park Service would stick to a legal or policy challenge," I said. "You know, focus on the fact that the state's predator control goal conflicts with the goal of wildlife management in the parks."

Maintaining an artificially high level of prey animals is incompatible with the purpose of the national parks, established in federal law, which is to preserve natural and healthy populations and processes. The management policies of the National Park Service prohibit the agency from doing anything that would reduce the number of native species for the purpose of increasing the number of harvested species in the parks.

Linda shook her head. "The national parks are for all Americans, not just for Alaskans and not just for hunters," she said.

John, a colleague who had lived in rural Alaska for forty years, heard us discussing the topic. "What's a few wolves? I don't mind if they kill a few."

I looked at him skeptically.

"There are plenty of wolves. Taking a few won't threaten the population," he said, shrugging.

"What they just did cut the wolf population in Yukon-Charley in half," I countered. "I guess I have a different interpretation than the state about what constitutes a 'sustainable population.'"

John looked almost apologetic. "You might not like it, but it's written in the state's constitution."

He was right. Reducing predator numbers not only aligns with the Alaska Constitution, it is mandated by it. The Alaska Constitution calls for managing wildlife according to the sustained yield principle and making wildlife available for maximum use consistent with the public interest. In 2003 the Alaska Board of Game, the state wildlife commission empowered to establish sport-hunting regulations in Alaska, had begun authorizing a number of measures to aggressively target predators. These included killing nursing black bear sows (aided by artificial light in dens), snaring black bears and brown bears (a snare trap is a length of cord with a noose at one end that strangles the bear when it puts its head through to get the bait), killing wolves during summer denning, and shooting wolves from helicopters and airplanes. These are all highly effective ways of killing predators.

"People have to eat," said John. "Lots of people can't just go to the grocery store. People living off the road system can't afford to buy all their food. They have to rely on moose and caribou, and if they can't get enough meat for the year, there are going to be real problems."

Alaskans do rely heavily on the bounty of wildlife in the state, and many residents feel that humans have not only the ability but also the obligation to manipulate natural systems to benefit people. The Alaska statute that's commonly called the Intensive Management Law says that animals like wolves and bears can be controlled to reduce competition with hunters for prey species like moose, caribou, and sheep so long as predator numbers are sustainable. By executing this law to its fullest potential, the state satisfies the needs and desires of many of its residents.

I also knew that many Alaskans feel that revenues from sport hunting, including hunts by non-Alaskans, are important to the economy and that it's imperative to keep predator numbers down to increase success of moose and caribou hunts. Many rural Alaskans, who are either involved in the sport hunting industry or who subsist off the land (or both) insist that predators are threatening their livelihood.

"And you think wolves and bears are killing too many moose and caribou?" Linda asked.

"Everyone in the bush says they're seeing more predators than ever," he responded calmly.

"That's interesting," I said, feeling myself getting worked up, "because Alaska Department of Fish and Game biologists I've talked to have found that animals have natural population fluctuations and natural shifts in migration that can make them harder to get to."

I also wondered if predator control actually achieved the intended results. One article I read said there was no legitimate scientific evidence that predator control actually decreases the number of predators and that sometimes it can have the opposite effect. For example, research showed that coyotes can have higher pup survival rates after culling, and mountain lions subject to predator control ended up expanding their ranges.

Another factor is that many Alaskans, including me, fundamentally object to killing wolves and specifically object to what we consider unethical means of doing so. Statewide surveys have found that Alaskans are divided on the issue, even in rural communities where some people feel that a manipulated playing field disrespects their relationship with wildlife. Many Alaskans are interested in boosting tourism and know that tourists come to see predators. Alaska statewide ballot initiatives passed in 1996 and 2000 limited aerial wolf control, but the Alaska legislature later reversed both initiatives.

"I'd rather kill 'em to make sure people aren't suffering," John said. "I don't get too sentimental about a few wolves."

What's wrong with getting sentimental about something I care about?
I thought.

I reflected on my trip with Shelley in the Arctic National Wildlife
Refuge. Though a year had passed, my favorite moment of that trip
was still clear in my mind. The preceding day we had hiked onto the
coastal plain, about to begin the final stretch toward the Beaufort Sea.
After the night had passed, it was a foggy morning, and we were snuggled in our sleeping bags. I had allowed myself to drift in and out of
sleep until hearing Shelley crawl out of the tent and turn on the stove.
I'd hoped she'd soon offer me a cup of hot tea.

After a minute, I heard the cellophane crinkle of rain pants running to the tent. Shelley pulled back the nylon door and whispered
excitedly, "Hey, come here! You'll want to see this!" We crouched in
the cool dampness beside the tent and watched the ghostly shape of
a wolf glide across the tundra. I don't know why I imagined the wolf
was female, but that's how I thought of her. She moved like an appa-
rition, a smudge of gray drifting in the fog. As she got closer she came
into focus, then caught our scent and glanced sharply in our direction. She was still as a statue. A whip of mist swirled around her legs.
There was no sound. Our eyes locked, and for a moment we inhabited
the same space. Due to the fog, nothing else existed. Then the wolf
turned away from us, her gray backside slipping into the cloud the
way a seal vanishes into the dark ocean.

I'd stared after her, unable to move. To see wolves ranging as they
always have, unhindered by humans. To unzip my tent in a morning fog and see a wolf move quietly as a cloud past my camp. I'd
felt myself unable to stop smiling. That wolf had gripped my spirit,
wrestled out a part of myself I'd forgotten about, connected me to
something mysterious and primal.

That had stuck with me, but it wasn't an easy thing to articulate
in a conversation about predator control a year later. "I just don't
feel what they're doing is ethical," I added to John, thinking about

the state initiating aerial shooting of wolves over large parts of Alaska and extending wolf hunting seasons ahead into late summer and back to spring (when the hides are of low quality and when pups are still dependent on their parents or are still in their mother's womb). The American Society of Mammologists, in addition to two hundred independent scientists, had recently written to Alaska's governor objecting to the state's predator control programs, which they felt were not ethical, biologically sensible, or even achieving the results desired by the state.

John gave me a shrug, and the conversation was over.

————

The wolves that the state killed were sometimes wolves my colleagues were studying, even though the National Park Service asked the state not to shoot wolves that had radio collars on them.

Every spring, biologists estimate the size of the wolf population in the six-million-acre Denali National Park. There are typically about eighty to one hundred wolves. In order to learn where the wolves move, what they eat, and how they die, researchers put radio collars on many of them, a process that requires pursuing a terrified wolf from an airplane or helicopter, darting it with a tranquilizer, and fastening a tight, bulky collar around its neck. From their offices, scientists monitor the collared wolves, and if a collar's signal indicates an animal hasn't moved for some time, they swoop down in a helicopter to locate the dead wolf. I deplored the methods used to collar wolves as much as I did the idea of wolves wearing collars, as if they were our pets, but the biologists said it was the only way park staff could understand exactly what it's responsible for managing.

One winter, biologists searched the frozen landscape from airplane and helicopter and collared as many wolves as they could. Understandably they were distraught when three wolves died shortly after being anesthetized.

I was disappointed too, because two of those wolves were from packs that ranged close to the park road, and I had yet to see a wolf in Denali. One of the wolves was from the East Fork pack, the pack named by Adolph Murie in 1939, Denali's most-adored pack, which often gives visitors a chance to glimpse one of Alaska's most iconic and elusive creatures. The dead wolves were sent north to Fairbanks where the necropsy found that they had heart lesions, which made them more susceptible to the effects of anesthesia. I imagined those three wolves, their hearts heating limp bodies sprawled on the snow, until ever so slowly the light went out and none of them woke up.

My colleagues wrote a press release explaining how the loss of individuals can affect local packs but wouldn't affect the larger population of wolves. I wasn't particularly comforted since the affected packs were the ones I was most likely to see. "Wolves are an important park resource," continued the press release, in case killing a few had created some doubt.

I looked up the definition of *resource*: a supply of something (such as money) that someone has and can use when it is needed; a source of wealth or revenue; a natural feature or phenomenon that enhances the quality of human life. The prospect of watching wolves had certainly enhanced the quality of my life, but it seemed like we tended to equate *resource* with *commodity* and measure wolves' value in terms of how well they serve us. Could we refer to wolves in a way that honors their right to live *for themselves*? After all, they don't struggle through winters and nurture their young so that tour companies can make a buck or to give hunters an interesting target.

Already I'd had to accept that hunting was a lawful activity in most of Alaska's national parks, but putting predators into a category of "wildlife resources" that humans get to cull and manipulate crossed a threshold regarding the sanctity of life. Instead of expressing my concern, I feared for my credibility in an agency accustomed to cataloging its resources. I was afraid that standing up for animals would make people lose respect for me. I was afraid they would think I wasn't a real Alaskan. Jaw clenched, I stood back and watched. I wanted to cry, not just for the pointless wolf deaths but also because no one around me seemed rattled. I didn't appear to be either. I masked my sadness and went about the business of writing about wolves as resources.

Later that winter, when the radio collars that had been fitted on a few other members of the East Fork pack indicated that the animals hadn't moved in a while, the biologists sure enough found them dead too. They concluded that they'd starved or fought each other to death. I could see them sometimes when I dreamed: tattered pelts and crazed yellow eyes, quivering noses and cupped ears, noses pressed to the snow manically tracing the scent of food.

At the end of that winter there were only a couple of members left in the East Fork pack. When I heard the news that one of them had wandered just a few miles outside the park boundary and stepped into metal jaws that clamped her front leg, I felt sick to my stomach. Trapping wolves is a legal activity outside the park's northern boundary, and pelts of wolves, wolverine, lynx, and martin are common décor throughout local neighborhoods. I wondered if, as the wolf's bones crunched in the jaws of the trap, she had suddenly felt lonely or whether she had already been lonely. As she wandered the tundra searching for food and a mate, did she know where the other wolves were? Caught in the trap, did she realize that this was the end for her?

A few years later, a local man would trap the alpha female of the East Fork pack. A necropsy would reveal that she had sat in his trap for ten to fourteen days, eating dirt and rocks. She lost 15 percent of her body weight and broke all of her teeth. I imagined her shaking with pain on the frozen tundra, blind with agony, tapping deep reserves of strength to survive. I imagined her finally letting her blood-soaked paw go limp and her head fall to the snow, waiting in a semiconscious state until footsteps approached. Then a deafening shot, the world going black, and her hot little heart freezing solid on the sled as the trapper rode home.

I cried for that wolf, but outside my group of friends I wasn't sure if I should mention how I felt. I watched how Alaskans drove past rows of animal pelts and huge swaths of logged trees and didn't flinch. What if I tried harder to be an Alaskan? What if I said these words out loud: *trees and animals are resources we need to use to get by up here on the final frontier.* I tried, but they tasted sour in my mouth.

At work after the news broke, it was a relief to see Page. "Disgusting," she said. She had tears in her eyes as she processed the details.

Like Page, I *wanted* to feel sad about the anguished death of a wolf. Being sad connected me to the wolf, and that's what I was after—to feel part of this extraordinary community of people and wild, intact ecosystems and all the life contained within them. Having emotions for a member of this community allowed me to feel like we were kin. Suppressing my feelings would have been like ignoring an ill family member.

———————

One night during my last summer working for Denali National Park, before I began working full time for the parks in the Northwest Arctic, I was biking the Denali Park Road. It was close to midnight, the buses had stopped running, and the tourists were tucked in bed. Denali, the mountain, was a crisp white silhouette against the blue-gray midnight sky. I stopped my bike when I saw moving shapes down on the gravel bar west of the Toklat River. Peering over the brush I counted three adult wolves and five pups romping around on the cobbles one hundred feet below. There was no one else on the road, so I stood in the pale light of the midnight sun and looked down at the braided bar winding through the tundra. A big black wolf glanced to the right and looked out over the pile of fur and ears and paws. The little ones clumsily tackled each other, nipped at each other's ears, and ripped at bits of flesh brought to them by the older members of the East Fork pack. Their world was cobbles and paws and midnight light along the edge of the big braided river.

Then suddenly I was stricken by the thought that these wolves could roam outside the park boundary and be trapped. What if they traveled to areas where the state's predator control efforts were underway? This wolf family could be chased across the tundra by snipers in airplanes and gunned down. Chilled, I pawed my way into a puffy jacket and kept watching.

It was easy to fall in love with Alaska while watching wolves in midnight twilight in Denali National Park. When I'd come to Denali that first summer, I hadn't considered growing roots in the far north, but I'd been collecting magical moments like pretty stones, and after a few years so many were weighing me down that it was difficult to imagine leaving. It was harder to imagine giving my heart to a state that stacked the bodies of dead wolves into shrines of irreverence. How could I reconcile my love and anger?

I refocused my attention on the scene below me. I felt like I was peering into the wolves' living room, like I was witnessing a private family ritual. I folded my arms across my chest to keep the heat in, and I thought about staying in Alaska. I wondered if I could simultaneously enjoy the grandeur and endure all the people and politics that continued to threaten what I loved most about this place. I stood at the edge of the gravel road, peering over the alders, and watched for a long, long time.

IT WOULD HELP TO HAVE A BOYFRIEND, MAYBE

In the fading winter daylight I watched Corrina move toward me in the middle of a wide snowy valley. It looked like the valley floor was scooped out the way an ice cream scoop carved one long shallow chute across the surface of a full tub of ice cream. Behind her the valley angled down until it touched the ice in Turnagain Arm three thousand feet below. There was a thick layer of clouds above the arm, as if the valley funneled the clouds downhill and spilled them over the ice. Corrina was tiny in this giant landscape, even in her puffy jacket and large backpack.

It was the inaugural race of the Hammer Adventure Racing series, concocted by Butch, Brij, and Becky to give us something to do in the mountains that was not quite as extreme as the famed Alaska Wilderness Classic but much more difficult than the plethora of orienteering, skiing, mountain running, and mountain bike races that occurred in and around Anchorage. They estimated that the route, which involved hiking, climbing, skiing, and biking on snow, would take teams between fifteen and twenty hours. The race route stayed close to town, the course designers having assumed correctly that the mountains around Anchorage feel even more rugged and remote in January than they do during summer.

At the start of the race Becky had stood before the small group of participants, who were bouncing up and down to stay warm at the starting line. "Although thirty miles might not seem long to some of you," she'd said, "It's going to be hard in the dark."

"It will be harder than you think," Brij had added with a mischievous chuckle.

That was fine by Corrina and me; we were looking to test our skills. I found myself signing up for races and ever-more-challenging wilderness excursions because I loved doing them. My passion for moving through wild country was growing into a defining energy that implored me to claim this place as my own.

As I watched Corrina en route and waited for her to take off one of her jackets, my nose hair froze, and I breathed shallowly, as if I had jumped into an ice-cold lake. The damp air smelled like a cave. Pink twilight saturated the snowy mountainsides. I was having a great time. It was exactly the kind of challenge I'd been hoping to face. Each race and wilderness trip over the last several years had been a stepping-stone for my confidence and sense of belonging. I held an image of a hypothetical Alaskan in my mind—homesteading and self-sufficient—and the image of a hard-core wilderness explorer.

Living up to either image would require extreme toughness, which I hoped to cultivate in myself.

Coworkers had begun to ask me what certain areas of the parks were like because they themselves had never been there. Friends asked me for gear recommendations and were interested to know what route through the Chugach I was contemplating next. When I signed up for this race, Butch smiled and said, "Look out, folks!"

There was nothing that made me happier than hearing that. My sense of self-worth and identity had become tied to these kinds of adventures, and it became addictive. It seemed like being labeled as tough was ephemeral, something I had to maintain, not something I would be stamped with for life after one or two challenging outings.

We hiked as hard and fast as we could across crusty snow. Then we post-holed through snowdrifts for hours, eating and drinking while we walked.

"So how's it going with Travis?" Corrina asked.

I winced and shook my head. "Looks like we're breaking up."

"Mmm. So sorry, A."

"It's hard to know for sure. I mean, how are you supposed to know when someone isn't good for you? When do you give up trying?"

Corrina is a counselor by training and says exactly the thing that makes me feel understood. "It feels like quitting," she said, and I nodded.

We walked side by side, now on cement-hard snow, and shared stories of recent boyfriends and why they didn't work out, and of my infatuation with good-looking, charming, outdoorsy guys. As I felt a stronger sense of belonging in my peer group and at work, I was intrigued by the next challenge—men who were doing more extreme outings than I was. Like all of my friends in Alaska—unattached twentysomethings and thirtysomethings—I was free to explore my attractions.

"Didn't we have the same conversation last year?" I said.

"Same story, different guys?" We laughed and hustled along, one foot in front of the other, turning our cheeks away from the wind.

I didn't need Corrina's professional assessment to recognize the danger. I'd put these talented athletes and adventurers on a pedestal, and if they rejected me it was going to crack the bedrock of my confidence. But I couldn't ignore laws of attraction, so it was an adventure I approached with some trepidation.

While the goal was never marriage, because that seemed unnecessarily serious, having a boyfriend seemed essential. I wasn't sure if it was because the chase and challenge and getting to know someone was simply thrilling, or if I was afraid of feeling lonely and less interesting without one.

"Maybe I don't need a relationship right now." I said the words aloud to see how they felt.

I expected Corrina to say "bullshit" and get me to tell her the truth—that having a hardcore Alaskan boyfriend would give me an even deeper sense of belonging, that partnering with an amazing athlete would, by association, elevate me to a new level of toughness and competence. Instead she raised her eyebrow skeptically and let me continue.

"Maybe I don't want a commitment. Why do I need a guy in my life when I have all this?" I made a sweeping gesture at the twilit silhouette of mountains. The mountains would be my strength. Their beauty my sustenance.

"What I've seen is that you don't want to *want* a boyfriend," said Corrina laughing. She turned to me, "I saw you checking out that tall guy at the start of the race."

I blushed. "Well, who is that guy anyway?"

"No idea. Never seen him before."

I thought about the guys I'd seen at parties, the guys in this race, at film festivals at the Beartooth, and at concerts at Moose's Tooth. They had strong, sculpted calves, ruddy cheeks, and messy hair. They were the fastest runners, the bravest climbers, and I was nervous talking with them. What if they rejected me? What if they didn't think I was that perfect combination of cute and tough? I wanted my self-confidence to stabilize and my childish yearning to be validated to be put to rest, but I couldn't be certain that I wouldn't hide from that tall blonde guy if I saw him again. What if I approached him and he turned away?

Our conversation distracted me from the cold and it meandered, delving into relationships with coworkers, feelings we had about living in Alaska, trip ideas, and finally looping back to boys and convincing one another that the next beautiful, alluring man we were both about to meet was going to be the one, even though we didn't actually need him.

About halfway through the race, it was close to twenty degrees below zero Fahrenheit. The teams were so spread out we didn't see anyone in front of us or behind us. We were about to descend the icy face of one of the Front Range peaks. Using headlamps to illuminate our feet, we kicked crampon spikes into the ice, rammed our ice axes into the crust, and leaned into the mountain. One kick at a time, very slowly, we dropped into the steepest part, like birds using talons to find purchase. The adrenaline surge warmed my skin and the darkness felt both comforting and deceptive; I couldn't see how far I might fall.

There is a balance that I know exists—when one is focused but not trying too hard, when there's grace and ease in the experience—but I couldn't settle into it.

When the slope eased, we found a packed trail that led us to the next checkpoint, where we traded climbing gear for skis. Too tired to talk, we listened to the rhythmic swish of our ski pants. On the downhill sections our skis scratched hard snow as we careened around corners. I stopped before the final steep descent, illuminated only by moonlight and the dim glow of city lights below. My cough broke the silence.

"Sweet," Corrina said. "Somewhere down there is the finish line." She used a big mitted hand to wipe a wisp of hair back underneath her hat. Her cheeks were like red coals, and her eyes smiled through foggy goggles.

"I don't know about skiing this one," I said, peering down the lick of steep snow. Neither of us were great at skiing.

"Watch out for the trees," she advised, shuffling side to side to keep warm.

I inched closer to the edge. "I might try to sled on my skis."

"Sure, go for it," she said, stepping to the side. "I'll give you some space."

I pointed my tips downhill, sat on the back of my skis, and shoved off. Quickly gaining speed, using my hands as rudders, I tried to keep my tips straight and not hit the bumps too hard. I was vaguely aware of trees flashing past, but at some point I closed my eyes and just felt myself flying. A second later the momentum diminished. At the bottom I came to a stop, righted myself, and looked back for Corrina. All I could see was the faint ball of light from her headlamp, jostled by snowy bumps as she careened down the trail.

She slid to a stop at my feet and then the night filled with her hearty, wild-girl laugh. I joined her because we were two of ten contestants in a city of three hundred thousand who desired to spend most of a day and night racing in the dark in freezing temperatures. I laughed because I belonged to this clan, and belonging gave me permission to do goofy things and feel invincible and free.

Corrina pulled herself up and bellowed, "Ha! They said we wouldn't be laughing after the first three hours, but we're twelve hours into it, and look, we still are!"

We hurried to the next checkpoint, where we traded skis for bikes.

I blinked to defrost the ice on my eyeballs as I biked toward the finish line. Shifting and braking seemed impossible with the hand warmers in my gloves and the heavy mitts over the gloves, so it was pleasantly surprising when those things actually happened. My helmet buckle was so tight over my hats and hoods that it was uncomfortable to swallow. No time for adjustments—we were on the home stretch.

At the finish line, Brij, Butch, and Becky cheered and high-fived and swept us into hefty hugs. Corrina and I smiled back—not the energetic smiles from earlier in the night but smiles all the same.

A few months later, the summer Hammer event was bigger and more challenging. This time Shelley was my partner, and over the course of fourteen hours we traversed the Talkeetna Mountains, negotiated glaciers and grizzly bears, scrambled over an obscure rocky pass, mountain-biked along the foothills of the Matanuska River, and arrived at the river's edge exhausted. The final leg involved pack-rafting the swift and wide Matanuska. I felt cold air rising from it. It was getting close to midnight and becoming too dark to see. We sat down in the dirt and licked soggy bread crumbs and almond butter from the inside of a plastic bag.

"Shit, girl," Shelley said. "What do you want to do? I have to say, boating this river in the dark scares the crap out of me."

I didn't love the idea either. "But we're close to the end, and I think we're in second place. We're beating all those teams of guys."

Which is why I wanted to jump in my boat, as scary as it would be. Shelley looked down, her brow scrunching. I knew she was thinking about the guys behind us, and her competitive streak didn't want them to close in.

She looked up. "Wanna go for it?"

I nodded. "You?"

"Let's do it." She raised her hand for me to slap, and we began inflating our boats.

As I gave my boat a few final puffs of air, I heard someone approaching. In an instant we heard Butch's familiar voice.

"Ladies," he said, "we need to talk." He sounded uncharacteristically serious. His face was somber. "We just pulled the lead team out of the river."

"What happened?" we asked wide-eyed.

"They hit a hole that flipped their boats, and they had to swim to shore in the dark. No dry suits."

I felt my throat tighten. They must have been freezing.

"They're pretty shaken up," he said, then added as an afterthought, "They're solid boaters too."

Butch adjusted his baseball cap and took a deep breath. "A different group called for a rescue on the hiking section. Some of the teams behind you are far less experienced. It's too much liability for us. We need to end the race here."

The following night at the post-race party at Moose's Tooth, I strategically chose a seat beside the tall guy I'd noticed at the winter race. He looked at me, and I smiled.

"Hi, I'm JT," he said, and then someone interrupted and asked him about a fifty-mile trail running race that he'd apparently done. I ate my pizza and listened.

JT had long blond hair and a casual way about him. He was cute, and I liked how modest he was about racing.

"Ah, I just got lucky," he said about winning the ultramarathon and the last Hammer race, even though no one else had come close.

The following week Corrina called me. "Hey, you know that guy from the race?"

"Uh, the cute guy?"

"Yeah. Well, he tracked me down at work. I guess he called a bunch of times, but I was never there. Anyway, he asked for your number."

"Really? We barely talked."

"Well, apparently you were memorable," she laughed.

JT and I met at the Prospect Heights trailhead for our first date. He pulled up in his purple pickup truck and let his enormous dog run over to me.

"That's Archimedes," he said as he closed the tailgate.

"Archimedes?" I said, thinking that was a peculiar name for a goofy-looking hound, tall as my waist.

"I teach high school math," he said.

The two of them were quite a pair: JT was six foot four, with legs up to my stomach. He and Arc loped along all legs and wind. JT's legs looked even longer in the purple spandex tights he was wearing. I laughed to myself. *Well*, I thought, *he's not constrained by fashion norms.*

The two of us, plus Arc, walked into the Chugach Mountains. We followed a trail until it forked, and then we took the steeper route that angled toward a ridge. I hiked as fast as I was able but couldn't keep a comfortable pace, so I avoided talking much by asking him questions. I was relieved when JT paused to call for Arc.

We scrolled through all the questions people ask when they're getting to know each other: where are you from, where is your family, what do you do for work, what do you like about living here. It turned out he was from the East Coast like me and he had gone to college in Virginia, just like I had.

"It seems like we've been on a parallel path," I said hopefully. "New Jersey and Pennsylvania, Virginia, Colorado, Utah, and finally Alaska. I can't believe we've lived in so many of the same places!"

He glanced at me, eyebrows raised. "It's uncanny. So what brought you here?"

"Bigger mountains and more space," I said, feeling a little flat-footed in my response. I was finding it hard to think when I couldn't catch my breath. "You?"

"I was looking for something more relaxed than the East Coast," he said. "I was looking for a different pace, different values, so I found

Girdwood, Alaska, and became a ski instructor, even though I didn't really know how to ski."

"You didn't know how to ski?"

"Yeah," he laughed. "I had just finished the summer working as a camp counselor at a summer camp so I knew a lot of games and group activities. It turned out it was a really crappy snow year in Girdwood, thank god. No one could ski yet, so the interview focused entirely on how to make skiing fun for kids, and I had all these ideas. I guess they just figured we all could ski or we wouldn't have applied for the job."

"So that was it," I said. "You found your place and your people and the rest is history."

"Not exactly," he said. "I was a ski bum for a couple years, then I went back to Utah because I felt like I needed a job with an income of more than $10,000 a year. I loved teaching in Utah, but I missed Alaska."

"It's different here," I panted as we crested the ridge.

"Yeah," he said looking around. "There's no place like it."

I asked him about his current job, and JT spoke excitedly and made broad hand gestures when he told me about the high school students that he taught. He did, however, admit to an ulterior motive.

"The best thing about being a teacher," he said with a smile, "is June, July, and August."

He asked what I did, and I told him I helped write management plans for the national parks. "Right now I'm working for Noatak National Preserve in the Western Arctic. I don't get the whole summer off or anything, but it feels good to help take care of these places."

His story reminded me of my own, and it seemed like the jobs we'd settled into did more than provide an income.

We sat an awkward distance apart on a flat rock on the spine of the ridge. I couldn't decipher what distance was appropriate—what distance, exactly, indicated that I was enjoying his company while acknowledging the fact that we barely knew each other? I sneaked glances at him when I thought he wasn't looking. I felt out of breath even though I wasn't moving.

JT broke the silence. "When we get back to the trailhead, if you're up for it, I have tickets to a concert tonight." The pitch of his voice rose. "We could grab dinner and go there, if you want to."

Little lightning bolts tickled every inch of my body. I didn't want the date to end, couldn't take my eyes off him. There he was, one of *those* guys. He'd waited until well into the hike to invite me to the concert, which either meant he was forgetful or he had decided he liked me.

TWO WORLDS

A few months later JT and I were hiking through the Chugach Mountains. We approached a knife-edge ridge with three-thousand-foot drops on either side. I tried not to imagine how far a person might fall over snowy cliffs before her body would come to a stop.

Because it appeared to be the slightly less terrifying option, I insisted we cross the snowfield below the ridge.

JT looked at me and raised his eyebrows, as if to ask why.

I felt like I could be honest with him. "I'm scared," I told him quickly.

The snowfield was fifty yards wide and hung above a band of cliffs that ringed the mountain. I kicked my sneakers into hard snow. It took about three kicks to carve a step that I trusted.

"Okay," he said, "I'll go first." JT strode across the snowfield, and I could tell he was trying to kick steps that I could follow. After a minute he glanced back. I'd seen that look of bewilderment before. I knew he couldn't understand how it could take this long, but if I told him I was sorry, he'd say it was perfectly fine, that it didn't matter how long I took.

My foot kept slipping, and I fought images of myself freefalling into oblivion. I squeezed my ice axe so hard I might have deformed the metal. JT made it to the other side then started walking back to reinforce the steps. The last time we had been crossing a steep slope I got mad at him because he kept going and didn't look back. I'd felt like he didn't care if I tumbled over the ledge. But this time I almost wished he'd keep going. I felt so angry with myself, so disappointed, that I forgot how cold I was. My hood was pulled up and I was focusing on my feet, but he saw me crying anyway. I thought to myself, *You think I'm crying because I'm scared, but really I'm crying because I wanted to make you proud.*

Adventuring with JT over the last few months had been nothing like exploring with Shelley, Corrina, Becky, or any of the women I headed into the wilderness with. I was accustomed to leading the way. On days spent backcountry skiing with my girlfriends, we often passed groups of men skinning up the mountain. They sometimes remarked that they didn't usually see a group of women skiing together, especially women who approached them from behind and waited for the guys to step aside so they could pass.

As I followed JT's steps in the snow, I thought back to the year my mom had flown to Alaska with a small group of her sixtysomething and seventysomething friends from Colorado to do a sea-kayaking trip in Glacier Bay National Park in Southeast Alaska. Our route had involved making two crossings of the West Arm, a total of four miles of open water. Unfamiliar with the dangers of paddling in Alaska—a sudden change in weather, a rogue motorboat, a calving glacier—the ladies had paddled on, mesmerized by the sunny day.

The marbled rock of the Fairweather peaks were shawled in shaggy green willow and alders. Waterfalls, like cascades of dashing light, coursed down from unimaginable heights. Steep rock walls climbed out of the icy turquoise fjord, and glaciers, rumpled with crevasses, spilled down to the water. Next to our kayaks, ducks skidded to a stop, creating miniature wakes on the glassy blue-gray surface. I gawked at the scenery as much as Mom's friends did, while Mom took every opportunity to compliment me in front of them.

"You probably see this all the time because you *live* here," Mom had said loud enough for everyone to hear.

I had seen the beauty, but I had also seen a lot of water between us and land. I knew that anything from a cruise ship to a storm could come out of nowhere, and I wasn't sure if they could get back in their boats if they fell out. If they couldn't get back in, there was no one around to help us, and none of them were wearing dry suits.

From camp, we'd paddled out toward the Lamplugh Glacier and watched big chunks of ice calve into the water. The water was thick with bobbing ice sculptures so we scooped small chunks into the kayaks for cocktails. As we angled closer to the glacier, the wind had picked up. Icy cold, it whipped the surface of the water into frothy little waves. With chilly fingers gripping our paddles, we pushed the plastic kayaks forward and heard ice grating their sides. The boats rocked precariously.

"Ladies!" I'd shouted over the splash of the waves. "I'm a little worried how rough it is here!"

"What do you think?" my mom had called over to the woman in the next kayak. "Do you want to turn around?"

The women had looked at one another and nodded in agreement.

Back at our beach camp, we had sat with the toes of our shoes pushed into the sand, cocktails in hand. Mom had turned to me, looking as content as I'd ever seen her. "This is the life, isn't it?" she'd said.

As I crossed the snowfield with JT and thought back to kayaking with my mom, I knew that if JT had been on that kayak trip he would have wanted to press on to the head of the inlet.

————

At the same time, there is a dynamic that I love about traveling in a group of experienced men. They assure me that it *will* work out, that we've chosen the right place to cross the snowy slope, that we *will* cross the river without falling in, that the boat *will* be aligned perfectly at the entrance to the rapids. My male friends are some of the most capable, creative, skilled people I've ever known, and I trust them. Sometimes, trusting them is all the power I have. Being in the group commits me to its will right from the start, even if the group's will is different from my own.

This dynamic often manifests on rafting trips, like the time I was rafting the Chickaloon River with JT and a couple of our male friends. When we stopped to scout a rapid, I stood behind JT and Todd and listened to them speculate about how the rafts would move through the gnashing part of the river in front of us. Next to the rapid I thought our boat looked pretty small, but Todd pointed to the boulder in the middle and said they'd just need to pull hard away from it.

I had no choice but to climb in and hold on. The river, after all, only goes in one direction.

The approach to the rapid gave me a chance to think about all the ways the raft might flip. JT used the oars to make slight adjustments to the raft's position as frothing holes loomed closer and closer and a roar filled my ears. I slid my fingers under the cinched straps on the seat and braced myself, and then all at once a fury of waves knocked the raft sideways as if we'd been T-boned at an intersection. Water splashed over my head, and I kept hanging on as we punched through, and finally there was one last hole so deep I thought we'd capsize, but JT had lined up the raft just right, and we slid just to the side of it. Calm water spread before us once again.

Life can feel like that too. Getting out of the river or making the current stop is not an option. Maybe that's what the Chickaloon trip taught me: sometimes I have to surrender to the moment, have faith in those around me, and embrace the mystery.

———

One snowy winter afternoon I was with JT, Todd, and Tony, kicking ski boots into the snow on the side of a steep, shaded gully in the Chugach, with skis strapped to our backpacks. The collar of my jacket was damp and icy, my neck was clammy, and my gloves were soaked. Wisps of frost-coated hair stuck to my forehead and cheeks. I pushed the hair back under my hat and focused on kicking my toes into the slope. I paused every ten steps to catch my breath.

Looming a thousand feet above us was an overhanging cornice that looked impassable.

"I don't know about that cornice," I said.

Todd looked up and squinted. "It should be fine."

"What if it avalanches on us?"

"We'll just get up there quickly," said JT, "and cut a hole through it."

The guys set their sights on the top, but I couldn't dismiss the trouble we'd be in if the snow broke free and fell on us. I reluctantly followed, my hands shaking when I looked down at the bands of rock that would grind my bones if I fell. I couldn't look up at the ceiling of snow looming overhead, threatening to crack and fall. I could only look at the metal buckles on my boots and kick one step at a time. I would have preferred an ice axe to a ski pole, and I would have been better off without a heavy, cumbersome load on my back. But there I was. Climbing up. I continued kicking one foot at a time into the face of the mountain and talked myself through it: *You got it. One more step. Good. One more step. Good. Don't look down. Focus. One more step.*

By the time I approached the top, the guys had cut through the cornice. A few more steps and I'd be there. The guys were right: the snowpack held. I hefted one foot up, then the other, through the cornice and onto the level, rocky ridge. The sweetest surprise was to discover I had done something that I never would have attempted on my own.

————————

The challenge for independent women who identify themselves as self-sufficient, athletic, and strong is to keep our confidence intact when we go adventuring with men who have more backcountry experience or a higher risk tolerance. Our confidence, and any other part of us that might be tied to that, is often tested on these outings. I was on a packrafting trip once in the Alaska Range before packrafts were ubiquitous and well-made. I had a Sevlor boat, essentially an inflatable forest-green bathtub prone to popping like a balloon, easy to submerge, and appropriate mostly for a child in a pond. The guys I was with had similar boats but more experience using them. It was the third day of the trip, the weather was starting to deteriorate, and the guys figured we could reach the road in one long push. "It looks like an eight-mile hike to the river and then a twenty-mile float back to the road," one of them said. "What do you think?"

I felt tired just thinking about it. "Seems like a lot, but I'll give it a try."

The river was splashy and shallow. I hit rocks that spun my boat in circles. I didn't have a dry suit, and my boat kept filling with freezing water. At first just my bottom was getting saturated, but then my feet and legs were too. I bent my knees, and they soon became the only dry islands south of my waist. At times, the guys were so far ahead of me that I couldn't see them. When I hit a shallow section and had to step out of my boat and carry it to a deeper channel, I was simultaneously relieved to get out of the water and panicked that I was falling farther behind.

At some point, after a few hours, I hit a gravel bar. I knew I needed to empty the water from the boat, but I just sat there for a time in my icy bath, fingers frozen around the paddle, legs too numb to move, eyes cold and blank. It was forty degrees and starting to rain.

I could just sit here for a little bit longer, I thought, *maybe close my eyes.* Maybe I would forget about the past three hours: How I'd almost gotten caught in a fallen tree that spanned the channel. How my foot had caught the tip of an alder branch and I was suddenly upside down in the icy water, seized by cold. How my boat had nearly popped as it was dragged along the ice of the riverbank. *Maybe if I sit here on the gravel bar there won't be anything else to be afraid of.*

I felt all the warning signs of hypothermia, but all that registered was the rain streaming down my cheeks onto wet rain pants. I tried making fists to wring the rain from my fleece gloves, but my hands were so cold that I couldn't seem to do it. And then I remembered that there was supposed to be a game trail beside this section of river. One that ran all the way to the road. I thought, *I can pack up the boat and find the trail. I have to move. I can't sit here. But I don't want to get up. Not yet. I just want to cry and go to sleep in my boat.* I counted to three and willed myself to get up. On three I didn't budge. I counted to three again, and with a grunt I lifted myself out. When I finally pulled the boat onto the bank, warm tears pooled in my eyes. I wasn't sure whether that was due to the sweet relief of knowing that I wouldn't have to get back in the water or whether it had to do with the impending embarrassment of having failed as a boater, of walking beside the river with a crumpled boat in my arms.

When Corrina is in her sea kayak and we are in the cold clear water of Prince William Sound, her paddle pulls through the water so smoothly it's as if she's stirring cream. The bow parts the turquoise water, leaving a wake of ripples behind her craft. Left, right, left, right, her strokes are perfectly synced, and the kayak moves straight as an arrow into the space between two big ice chunks. She silently notes the occasional seal head, the chunk of ice from the calving glacier, the contour of the land to our right, and I see it too without her having to point it out. Her deliberate paddling is an elegant dance on top of the water's surface. Her tiny figure buoyant in the boat is a delicate complement to the immense landscape. It is as if she was meant to be there with the bear tracks on the sandy shore, the kittiwakes cartwheeling along the cliffs, the seaweed floating through cold transparent water beneath her. As I paddle behind her, I think about how women in wilderness easily embody such grace.

One evening on a ten-day trip in the Arctic with Becky, the two of us reflected on our day. It had been a good stretch of paddling, and the Arctic had revealed more treasures than usual. That afternoon we'd seen three bears, their backs blond from the never-setting summer sun, an Arctic fox, and a group of caribou, all before it had started raining.

We cinched open the large door of the floorless tent so that we could enjoy the view of the river. Rain pattered the tent, and the walls billowed inward during strong gusts of wind. After a five-hour paddle, avoiding exposed rocks in the shallow rapids, and finding a camp on a level bench above the water, we sat there with our million-dollar view, full after a hot dinner, snuggled in dry clothes, each of us with a thermos of hot tea and a pair of binoculars beside our books.

Two girls canoeing through the Arctic, a hundred miles from anyone. And in that moment I reclaimed the confidence I had lost in the Sevlor raft and crossing steep snowfields with JT.

Not only does it feel good to be part of a group of self-sufficient women in the Alaskan wilderness and to do something that a lot of men don't have the courage or ability to do, there is also tremendous satisfaction in the way we approach trips. Our approach is less goal-oriented and more focused on enjoying the day, making sure everyone is happy.

We know we're going to have fun. And we know there will be no pressure at all. I know I won't have to prove anything or feel afraid of failing.

I look around more often. I notice the details. The result is a more harmonious experience, an exchange between the wilderness and us, rather than us going into the wilderness to conquer something.

Over the years, my girlfriends and I have relished the trips we've done together. We have loved the dynamic we created. We have loved feeling empowered and at ease. But we still had to learn how to manage our egos on trips with our boyfriends and husbands.

I had to understand that JT wanted to do trips with me. Maybe he did them with me because he thought I was capable, and maybe he did them with me because he enjoyed my company even if I couldn't move as quickly as he could. Either way, he thought that I was enough, but it took a while for me to feel that way about myself. I had to learn how to cross a steep, icy slope one foot at a time and sincerely thank JT for kicking such nice steps for me. I also had to learn that when JT crossed that icy slope and didn't look back to see if I'd made it across too, he was showing how strong and capable he believed I was. I had to learn to not equate such apparent indifference with callousness. I had to learn that it was a compliment. I had to learn how to navigate both worlds.

THE EDGE

The following summer JT and I flew across Cook Inlet where the Alaska and Aleutian Ranges come together in a fury of spires and cliffs and glaciers tumbling down mountainsides. The Cessna 206 landed on floats and delivered us to the shore of Telaquana Lake at the foot of the jumble of peaks. Our packs were heavy with eight days of food, harnesses, crampons, rope, carabiners, prusiks, packrafts, paddles, dry suits, helmets, and a life jacket for each of us. It was an unreasonable load for JT, who was carrying almost twice as much as I was. It was also an unreasonable load for me, since two weeks earlier when I was recovering from swine flu I had been hit by a car while riding my bicycle. I had a pretty severe concussion for ten days and a bruised, swollen hip, but then I felt good enough to walk and was up for an adventure.

JT and I had been dating for over a year. He knew me well enough to know that this trip might end up being too big a challenge for me, and because it was so remote he was reluctant to commit to it. I begged him. "There's no one else I trust to do this with."

He saw how much it meant to me and gave me a sincere smile. "Okay," he said. "Let's do it then."

Since I'd crossed the threshold from my twenties into my thirties I at least *liked* to think I had a better idea when someone was good for me. I'd found that JT always showed up for his friends, and he showed up for me, even in my most vulnerable moments. I'd witnessed how he carried more of the shared gear on backcountry trips, how he surprised everyone with chocolate bars after dinner, how he brought far more to potlucks than he needed to, and how he usually volunteered to drive. His agreeing to this trip was an extension of that generosity. So off we went to begin a trek that no one, as far as we could determine, had ever done before.

Soon into the hike we were clawing at brush so thick that we were able to travel only about a half mile per hour. Anxious to free myself from the web of alders, I waded into the icy creek without even bothering to roll up my pants. I felt the gushing current pushing me off balance, so I reached out to hold JT's hand, and together we took slow, tedious steps over the slippery rocks. After a minute we leaped out of the creek, cursing the stinging cold. Walking in the creek was no faster or less painful than the alders, but at least it was different.

Back in the brush we wriggled and kicked and wrestled our backpacks from the branches. Our route was supposed to take us up that drainage, over a pass, down the other side, up a glacier, over a glaciated pass, and down the other side onto another glacier, where we would, we hoped, find a way off the glacier and onto the river coming out of it. With any luck we would be able to use our little inflatable packrafts to float the river all the way to Lake Clark.

"What kind of bushwhack would you call this?" JT yelled over his shoulder. He knew I liked to make up names for miserable experiences.

"Body-shwack," I said irritably. Lurching all my weight into an alder still wouldn't make the alder let me pass.

JT was moving faster than me, and soon I couldn't see where he went. Running into a bear in this brush would have been terrifying. For a while we'd yelled "Hey bear!" constantly, but that had waned to sporadic shouts.

"Hey, where are you?" I yelled. I stopped and listened. I could hear brush moving up ahead and a little to the right. I banked on it being human body-shwack, not that of a bear, so I angled toward it.

Have patience, I told myself, although patience has never been something I've had much of.

One of the things weighing down my pack was the latest edition of my favorite literary magazine (in case we got weathered in somewhere). As I lunged at an alder, something I'd already read in it came to mind, an interview with author Malidoma Somé, a native of Burkina Faso. Somé believes that people who face challenges in nature often get rewarded for their suffering. As I extracted my elbow from two branches, his words gave me a bit of motivation to push on. In the interview Somé spoke about formal initiation rites that are found throughout the world, where the initiate must go into wilderness and face a significant challenge in order to gain insight into their life purpose. Often the initiate may nearly die or at least feel at mortal risk but then transcends the challenge and is changed forever. From then on, the initiate carries something powerful within.

In the middle of the alder thicket, when I couldn't see anything but green serrated leaves in every direction, it was hard to recognize that the alders were trying to teach me patience and perseverance. Not totally receptive to Somé, I panicked and wondered if the alders would ever end. I angrily whacked the branches, wishing I was stronger, berating myself for choosing that route. But I was also more determined than ever to get to the other side of the pass.

Eventually JT and I found a bear trail that led to a series of gravel bars, and from there we ambled to the first pass. I let my heavy pack thud to the ground and propped myself against a boulder to admire the view of nameless mountains all around.

"Did you read that Somé interview?" I asked JT.

"Yeah, about the initiation rites."

"Can you think of anything like that in our culture?"

"Nothing like what he was talking about," he said. "Not where we send people into the woods for vision quests."

"This is probably as close as we get," I said.

JT sipped water and reflected. "When I'm out here, I feel like I'm doing what I'm meant to do. It's not always that deep. It's not like there's this big revelation, but something feels right inside, especially after I've figured out some difficult part of the trip."

I nodded. I don't have an epiphany about the meaning of my life every time I have a difficult adventure. "There was the gift of the bear, though," I said, remembering an earlier outing, with Brij and Butch.

One morning in the Brooks Range, Brij, Butch, and I had spotted a shaggy brown mass humping over willows in a direct line toward us. We stopped, frozen, and waited. A large grizzly trundled over a rise in front of us and continued running in our direction. My heart pounded. My breaths became quick and shallow. The three of us bunched together. We had no gun, no pepper spray. There were no rocks or sticks in sight.

We yelled at the bear, then at each other, "Stay closer together! Brij, you're *filming* this?"

Thirty yards away the bear stopped, and we screamed, "Go away! Get the hell out of here!"

It reared up on its hind legs.

"Maybe it knows we're humans now," Brij whispered in a shaky voice.

For a moment I thought it was going to turn away, but the bear dropped back down to all fours and resumed swaggering toward us. My hands trembled. "Damn it, Butch, stop backing up!"

Closer and closer until it closed the gap to about ten yards. Still we stood our ground. It looked right at us, strands of saliva streaming from its muzzle.

"Louder, scream louder!" I yelled.

We waved our arms. It circled us, slowly. Then, finally, it decided we weren't worth it.

Without a doubt, that bear could have killed us if it had wanted to. You might call it a brush with death. You might call it an initiation. Whatever you call it, since that morning, the three of us have referred to that moment as "the gift from the bear." We speak of the encounter with reverence.

Shortly after that trip I had been invited to give a talk at the Alaska Public Lands Information Center in Anchorage, and I'd jotted down idea after idea, most of them too sentimental, too overdone for a talk to cruise ship tourists, but I kept at it, typing, deleting, reworking. I'd been determined to convey that seeing predators in their natural setting can be a life-changing experience and that it's important to continue protecting public land so that we have intact ecosystems in the United States. There are not many countries left that do. In writing, I'd felt that bear's hot breath behind my ear. *Get it right*, he whispered. That must be what Somé means when he talks about undergoing a trial in order to gain insight into your purpose in life and how to share your passion with the world. The gift of the bear, in part, was the affirmation that I was on the right career path, moving toward an even greater respect for wild places and animals. The encounter led me to believe that it is a good and honorable thing to speak up for the land and the creatures who cannot.

Steadying ourselves under our packs once again, JT and I headed down the other side of the pass toward the headwaters of the Neacola River. Less than an hour later I gave a quiet cheer as I ditched my backpack for the final time that day and began to pitch our tent on the last patch of tundra before everything became rock and ice. We sat across from each other and ate reconstituted chicken stew. The ground felt luxuriously smooth and cool on my wet, wrinkled feet. I handed JT a cup of tea and then hugged my own hot cup to my chest.

The following day we climbed up onto the glaciers that melt into the Neacola River. Bear and wolf tracks crisscrossed the snow. As the sun warmed the day, the snow on the steep mountain walls above the glacier began to melt and release thunderous waves. Avalanches collapsed down the vertical rock walls, white waterfalls of snow and ice. Each cascade echoed throughout the immense valley as we slogged through wet, shin-deep snow. This was unchartered territory for us, and I was feeling a little nervous about what lay ahead, but JT looked up and said, "Let's go! I can't wait to see what's up there!"

I followed his quick steps up the wide river of ice and snow. Every now and then we paused to drape ourselves over our backpacks like towels drying in the sun. We let our eyelids feel the heat, let our ears fill with quiet. At the end of the day we made camp in an amphitheater of rock and ice. Our socks and shoes, soaked from trudging through wet snow all afternoon, dried on a little patch of rock under the strong evening sun. By late evening, everything that hadn't dried in the sun quickly began to freeze. An aching cold settled over our camp, and we retired into our sleeping bags, spread over our packrafts for extra insulation. All around us were mountains that had never been climbed, peaks without names.

I nestled in close to JT and wrapped my arms around him. "Thank you," I said.

"For what?" He looked at me strangely.

"You know," I said, not making eye contact, "everything." I suddenly felt too vulnerable to elaborate. It was his competence on this type of trip, his calm under pressure, that I loved most. His confidence helped me remember to take challenges one at a time. His lighthearted manner tempered my occasional impulse to feel overwhelmed. Too embarrassed to say these words, I hugged him instead.

"You're so weird," he said, and he hugged me back.

I closed my eyes, and all that came to mind is that I loved being out there. These wild places draw out our true character: they allow us to see what we're made of and discover what type of person we want to be. I like who JT is in the wilderness. I like how our lives swirl together out here, like the confluence of two rivers.

As the weight of sleep closed in, I thought about how nice it had been to have a partner—and not just on this trip. Did I have the courage to admit I was actually thinking about marriage? After all, one of my tenets was *Don't rely on anyone to take care of you.* But I needed a companion out here to help ward off bears, to navigate with me, to help me cross the rivers. It was fun to witness JT's excitement and to share the joyful moments. Wouldn't it be nice to have that kind of companionship not just on trips but also in the broader adventure of life? What if I reframed my conviction? What if I was not depending on JT but partnering with him, sharing companionship?

JT hadn't mentioned marriage, and I wondered if it had crossed his mind. Marriage would be a big leap. It would be like jumping off a cliff and trusting that we'd land on something soft. Normally nervous around cliffs, I was surprised that this time part of me felt propelled toward the edge.

———

The next day as the sun melted the early-morning ice crust, we punched through two feet of fresh snow on the glacier. JT inflated his packraft and loaded his gear in it, pulling it behind him like a sled. In a few hours we were up and over the pass. Our friend Dan Oberlatz had shared information about the area up to this point, but neither he nor local adventurer Cash Joyce had been down the other side, and so probably no one in recent history had.

Traversing the upper part of the glacier felt easy compared to the bushwhacking. Sunshine warmed us as we tramped through

increasingly wet snow. As the sun baked the mountainsides, avalanches tumbled down huge shields of rock that lined the sides of the
valley. We carefully walked closer to the center of the valley floor.

We were approaching the edge—the edge of the glacier and the
place in my mind where I hesitated for a moment and doubted my
ability. Many people seek experiences more extreme than this one and
have edges that require taking risks far greater than we were playing
with. I knew that my edge didn't require me to push into that much
unknown, so it was with trepidation that I walked past ice-scratched
fins of rock along the North Fork Glacier. Glaciers have a way of
cracking and tumbling at their terminus, rendering them challenging
to pedestrians.

As expected, near the end of the glacier, the snow vanished and
exposed endless hills of cobbles, boulders as big as trucks, and steep
ice walls. The glacier was not going to tenderly set us down onto the
valley floor. Immediately our route was like the mouth of a lion that
needed a lot of dental work. As the sun cooked the moraine, rocks
melted out of the ice and crumbled down around us, falling dangerously close as we picked our way over boulders resting precariously on
icy slopes. For a mile, I concentrated on each step and caught myself
praying for stable footing. We still weren't sure there was a way down.

"Not looking good, is it?" I called to JT.

"Yeah, we'll find out."

"It's going to suck if we have to hike all the way back."

"Do you want to take a break?" he asked.

I worried about it getting late and having to backtrack. "Thanks.
I'm okay for now."

We climbed up a ridge of rubble that abruptly cliffed out. We
backtracked and looked for another way around. As we scrambled
up and down the hills of the moraine, I stopped thinking about the
end. I retreated deep within myself to reservoirs of strength I hadn't
tapped in a long time. JT and I didn't speak. I wondered if I ought to

talk to him about what we would do if we couldn't get down. I considered telling him that I didn't have the strength to make it back up the glacier—I had been rock-hopping for hours over unstable rocks with a fifty-pound backpack after already hiking for nine hours. But I said nothing. My silent mantra became "a little bit farther."

Finally we were close. We could see the end of the glacier, but as we wandered around and peered over edges, we didn't see a clear way down the fifty-foot-tall toe. We traced the perimeter for a while. Then, among the icy cliffs, JT spotted it—a ramp of loose rock that led down to the valley floor and an oval of sand large enough for our tent.

"Right here!" he shouted, and I hurried over.

I was so delighted with JT, so proud of him for his patience and calm perseverance. I never would have made it without him. Maybe, just maybe, being able to count on someone isn't such a terrible thing.

Twelve hours after leaving our camp that morning, we pitched our tent near an ice cave where water gushed from the glacier to form an energetic North Fork River that appears to wind for miles through rocky moraine. Our tent marked the spot where the glacier starts to shed its rocks in big, loose, jumbled piles the way a snake might wriggle out of its old skin. As I lowered myself to the ground to begin cooking dinner, I glanced over at JT, who was organizing our gear. Replaying the day in my mind made me grin. We had been a great team that day, and there was no one else I'd rather be with.

The next day we inflated the boats, and JT knew that I was nervous.

"How freaked out do you think you're going to be today?" he said playfully.

"I'm up for it, but you know—" I looked down the river. "It's fast with those tight corners. We don't know if there's going to be a rocky sieve or a waterfall around the bend."

"So," he said, pretending to do the math in his head, "how many boxes of Kleenex is it going to take to wipe up all your tears today?"

I pretended to knock him over with my kayak paddle.

JT led the way. It was fast and splashy. I bounced off rocks and hit holes, and my boat filled with water every five minutes in spite of its spray skirt. For six miles I focused on nothing but the path of water off the bow of my boat. Every few minutes I reminded myself to relax my shoulders. And sometimes, when I bounced over a rapid and my boat didn't even come close to flipping, I realized that I was smiling.

The river pulled out of the tight moraine into an open, braided gravel river. Green forest lined the banks, and hanging glaciers and waterfalls cascaded down walls to the valley. I slouched in my boat and let out an audible sigh.

We spent the next few days letting water and gravity do most of the work, floating the Tlikakila River back to Lake Clark. I returned home with the souvenirs of a sunburned nose and hands cracked from icy glacial water, buoyed by an unparalleled sense of accomplishment. I walked purposefully. I was able to focus on one conversation at a time. I noticed colorful veins in rocks. I heard individual birds. The majority of things I normally thought about had been stripped away, the self-doubt scoured like the boulders beneath a retreating glacier.

I thought back to the interview with Somé. An extreme event, such as nearly dying, isn't a prerequisite for me, but a wilderness setting is. It is there where challenge and mystery slip in beside me, take hold of my wrist, and guide me toward the edge.

ROOTS

It was an October weekend, early in the morning. JT and I were living together in the log home that he built in 1998 in the mountains above Eagle River. I was lying on the futon on the floor, trying to clamp the cotton comforter around my neck without actually waking up. JT kept moving, and every time he did, a little heat escaped. I wondered why he was awake so early.

As he slid from the covers he whispered, "Why don't you stay in bed. I'll go downstairs and make you breakfast."

I dozed off, expecting JT to wake me with tea and a bagel, but when I awakened I realized he hadn't returned. In fact, there was no noise whatsoever in the kitchen. No indication that any breakfast was being made. I told myself to be patient, not to ruin it, that he had probably just gotten distracted.

After an hour it seemed suspiciously quiet, so I peered out of the bedroom and walked downstairs. I stepped slowly and held on to the staircase's wooden railing as I scanned the living room. On the table I noticed a dozen roses in a vase, with a walkie-talkie and a note nearby that said, "I told you I'd make you breakfast, but I didn't say where. Head outside and up the mountain."

My heart raced. *Why did I wait so long?* I dashed into the oversized gear room, rummaged through a Rubbermaid bin to find a wind jacket, and pulled a sweatshirt over my pajamas. I laced up one of the pairs of old sneakers that were piled in the corner by the door and took off across the driveway and into the woods.

I jumped when the walkie-talkie crackled: "Where are you?" JT's voice was a bit playful.

"Um, hiking up behind the house," I said, as I dashed toward the faint path of beaten wildflowers that led from his house to the treeless tundra. We call this place Threebowls because there are three distinct bowls, or gullies, that funnel down to the house. I scanned the swatch of mountainside in front of me and didn't see anything unusual. "Where are *you*?" I asked.

"Head toward Picnic Rock," he instructed.

In five minutes I reached the big flat boulder on the edge of the ravine. We call this spot Picnic Rock because it's the first good rest stop above the brush before the tundra-covered bowls come into view. "It's starting to rain harder," I told him.

"It's raining?" he asked.

"It's not raining where you are? Where are you?" I shouted, laughing into the speaker.

"Look up to the top of the ridge," he said. "I'm waving at you."

Sure enough, I could make out a person standing at the very top. My pajama pants were soaked from the brush, but I didn't feel the slightest bit cold. I was breathing much harder than normal and couldn't seem to catch my breath. The roses, the note, the chase—there was only one reason I could think of to explain this. But what if it wasn't that? What if this was just for fun? I didn't want to get my hopes up.

Rain turned to slushy drizzle, and my ragged sneakers slipped as I clawed my way up. Was there any reason I *didn't* want this to be what

I thought it was? I had spent most of my life swearing that I wouldn't be tied to anyone, dependent on anyone. I scanned my emotional self for any sign that those old thoughts were loitering around, but I found no trace of them. It seemed actually *better* to have someone to share this life with. Dating is exhausting. For the first time I thought, *I choose stability.*

After forty-five minutes of hiking I realized that JT had been telling the truth—it was not raining at the top. It was snowing but only lightly. I stepped up onto the ridge where JT was waiting. Eagle River Valley below and the wide, open expanse toward Denali to the north were faintly visible.

JT embraced me. I felt my flushed cheek against his cold, wet jacket. Looking up at him expectantly, I couldn't think of anything to say. Everything felt as though it was happening in slow motion.

"Come here," he said, and he took my hand. He led me along the ridge about twenty yards to a rocky outcrop, the high point on this end of the ridge. My heart galloped. JT turned to face me and knelt down on the rocks.

"I can't imagine my life without you," he said. He beamed, blue eyes shining, and looked hopeful as a puppy. "Will you spend your life with me?"

I was too nervous to absorb all the words, but it did register that this was a marriage proposal.

I pulled him up into my arms. "Yes, I love you," I said smiling. He smiled just as broadly. Awash in relief, I wrapped my arm around his waist and he steered me to the tent that he'd set up. Indeed, he had prepared breakfast: chocolate muffins, dried mangos, truffles, strawberries, and a bottle of champagne. What had just transpired couldn't be followed with conversation, so we huddled over the spread of food and grinned at each other. I shivered in my wet pajamas and noticed that he was shivering too (after all, he had waited up there for an hour while I was lying in bed).

The planner in me couldn't contain my excitement. Eventually I asked, "When should we get married?"

"Next summer?" he suggested.

"Sure, how about August?"

We tasted every sweet, chocolaty morsel JT had hauled up there, and we toasted our future with champagne between each bite, happy, hopeful, absorbing every second of that morning. At 10:00 a.m., drunk on champagne and chocolate, we slid down the mountain through sleet-covered fireweed and hellebore to call our families.

———

The following spring, the snow smelting, JT and I were ready to begin another summer of exploring. We met after work one Friday and set out hiking from the Eagle River Nature Center, about five miles from our house as the raven flies, with camping gear and the dogs. We walked six miles on the trail beside Eagle River, which was flowing low since its ice coat had just melted. The turquoise river looked sparkly and fresh as it braided across the wide valley.

Just past Dishwater Creek we left the trail and bushwhacked across a spruce forest with an understory of prickers. We'd been here before and knew that if we got lucky and found the good route, we'd only have to bushwhack through low brush, but if we chose poorly we'd end up prying back heavy spruce boughs and clambering over a snarl of fallen trees and devil's club stalks. This time we chose poorly.

At the edge of the valley, where the terrain got steeper, we kicked our way into a gravelly gully and clawed through prickly bushes and loose rocks until we reached the first cliff band. A faint trail cut through the rocks to a swatch of mostly flat ground hemmed in between cliffs, where we camped. It took us just three hours and cost me only a few thorns in my palms to get there.

Mountain goats seemed to hang like white ornaments on the cliffs above us.

"Look, there goes one!" I shouted as a goat leaped ten feet up to a rocky perch that couldn't have been more than a foot wide. We watched wide-eyed and listened to the crash of rocks, dislodged by goat hooves, trundling down the cliffs. I'll never cease to be in awe of a creature packed with such power and precision and imbued with the confidence to disregard a possible thousand-foot freefall.

From camp we looked down onto the winding river and up a massive rock face rising on its other side. Behind us, the peaks of the Icicle Creek drainage glowed in dimming sunlight—not too shabby a view after spending all day in the office.

That evening we tensed as five black bears angled in toward our camp one at a time. Eventually, after monitoring them for a while, we said to hell with it and went to sleep. The dogs would let us know if one got too close.

The next day we struck out toward Icicle Peak. The morning felt crisp and fresh as we crossed a mountainside that plunged over a cliff to the valley. We contoured around the side of the mountain, bushwhacking through alders and crossing gullies filled with snow. The previous day's cycle of thawing and refreezing had slicked the snow with a layer of ice, so we strapped metal micro-spikes onto our shoes to traverse the gullies. JT hopped along as if it was nothing, while I cautiously kicked the spikes into the ice and used a stick for balance in case I slipped. When I looked up I saw JT taking photos of me and laughing.

"I swear I'm going to kill you if you take a picture right now," I said, bending over the stick again.

"What? Me?" he said playfully. "I'm just capturing this thrilling moment."

"Seriously. This is steep!" I shouted. "I could fall and die right here."

"I like your technique with the stick," he said. "Do you think you could bend over a little more?"

I stopped and looked up at him. "Did I really agree to marry you?" I asked. "Is it too late to change my mind?"

"Sorry, sister," he said smiling, "You're stuck with me."

Despite the heckling, I was glad he was waiting for me. Trusting that JT cared about me had helped me accept my own abilities. I was not ashamed of my walking stick or the speed at which I was moving.

We finally arrived on the valley floor and rock-hopped up the boulder-strewn cascade.

"This is a lot of work to get to a point where it starts being fun," I remarked.

He rolled his eyes as if to say "it's not so bad" and leaped across a boulder. I crawled over it, rolling my eyes at JT's rolling eyes, but by that point he and the dogs were too far ahead to see. That day I let them go and just plodded along at my own pace. I felt joyful about the emerald moss and orange and black lichens growing on the sides of the boulders. I felt delightfully steady as I balanced on a tree root beside the creek. The root, the tree, the creek, the glacial moraine we were approaching, my trust in JT—they were my anchors.

Our reward came as we stood at the base of Icicle Glacier. Its firm coat of snow invited us to walk right up. On a steeper pitch, the glacier had cracked open as it rolled over a lip. We kicked steps in the snow beside gaping blue crevasses and kept going until we were at the head of the valley. It was just the two of us and the two dogs way back there with Icicle, Old Soggy, and Yukla Peaks boxing us in. The only place left to go was up.

It was a blissful, sunny afternoon, hot in the reflective snow. We wore short-sleeved shirts and lathered sunscreen onto salt-crusted skin. After the long dark winter it was hard to believe it felt so much like summer.

"So," said JT, "I've been thinking about where we could have the wedding."

"Yeah?" I said, delighted that he'd been giving it some thought. The idea of planning a wedding felt overwhelming, and I knew I'd end up relying on him for much of the work.

"What would you think about getting married in the Chugach?"

Smiling as I kicked steps up the face of Icicle Peak, I thought about getting married in the mountains. It made perfect sense. Mountains and the promise of beauty and growth drew each of us to Alaska. We fell in love in these mountains, and they provide the backdrop for the house that JT built, which we both call home. The mountains inspire common values that bind us together with a community of friends who hail from places as varied as the Deep South, New England, the Midwest, New Zealand, India, Austria, and England. I feel tied to this place more than to any other place in the world.

About the time my toes started to feel bruised from kicking running shoes into the glacier, dark clouds suddenly amassed over the peak. Once I would have forced myself onward, but I'd sensed a self-transformation. I took a deep breath.

"Honey," I said. "You should go ahead. I don't want to make you wait for me if our weather window is closing."

"Really? You're just a couple hundred feet below the summit. Are you sure?"

"Yeah, this has been great," I said. "I'm totally satisfied. I climbed Icicle Peak good enough." And I discovered that the words felt true. I was genuinely happy with the climb.

JT turned to face me and tilted his head. "But you won't get to the top," he said emphatically. I knew he didn't understand how a person could lack the drive to reach the summit. I'd been unable to make him see that, unlike him, I'm not haunted by peaks I haven't stood atop.

"I got as far as I wanted. I'm happy. You, on the other hand," I said, "you should go."

"Thanks, Love." JT took off at a strong clip, and I headed back down the face, one foot at a time. The mountains, I reflected, had also provided the setting and the opportunity for me to learn a little more about who I am. On the brink of committing to a lifelong partnership with JT, I was realizing that I didn't need to prove anything to myself or to him. He wasn't going to love me less if I didn't climb a mountain. I climb (or partially climb) mountains because they are my home. My heart is never more at peace than it is in these hills, and that moment of accepting my own limits was no exception.

———————

It was a Sunday in late June and I was pacing around the house. I walked through the bedroom where I'd left the bed a tangled mess. I glanced in the bathroom. It was time for lunch when I realized I'd been moving from room to room under the pretense that I might clean something. I didn't feel like cleaning. What I wanted was for JT to come home. I went downstairs to make lunch. Sitting in front of a turkey sandwich, I stared at the final wedding to-do list that JT had written three days earlier, before he left to climb that big mountain.

I called Becky. "He should be home by now," I said.

"When did he say he'd be back?" she asked.

"This morning."

"Well," she said, "I know it's hard, but he's not that late yet."

"I know." I remembered JT imploring me to always give him twenty-four hours past his projected return to find his own way out. "I wouldn't worry except that he's *always* ahead of schedule. He always calls by now."

She didn't say anything so I added, "He's the guy who shows up ten minutes early no matter what we're doing. He finishes races an hour before he says he expects to. He consistently overestimates the time it will take to do anything. Do you see? This situation, it's not right."

"What are you going to do?" Becky asked.

"I don't know. Eat chocolate chip cookies and worry, I guess."

God damn it, I thought as I hung up the phone, *will you just fucking get off that mountain?*

I contemplated going for a hike but knew I'd just obsess over the possibility of missing a critical phone call. As I checked the clock again, I was suddenly aware of the irony—I'd coveted the adventure lifestyle without fully recognizing the risks that came with it. I'd understood that superficially, but only then with my untouched turkey sandwich in front of me and phone in hand did I realize the true impact of loving someone who was unaccounted for in the mountains.

Later that afternoon I called a friend who lived near the trailhead, and asked him to look with his telescope for a climber on the peak across the valley.

I heard him drag the telescope to a window, and then there was a pause. I imagined him focusing on the massive peak enveloped in snow and ice. "I don't see any movement on the snow shield below the summit," he said, "but the top is socked in. I can't see anything on the summit."

"Okay," I said, "Thanks for checking."

"Looks rough up there," he added. And then, after a moment, "Do you have a plan?"

"I was hoping you would offer me one."

"Well," he stalled, "you know, the snow's exceptionally deep this year. Who knows what the river crossing is like right now. The steep pitches at the top are probably covered in ice. Lots of unknown variables. Hard to make a call."

"Maybe he's just delayed in the storm. Maybe he had to bivy up high, or maybe his ski broke or something," I offered.

"Call me later if you hear anything or if you want me to check again."

I checked email. I painted my toenails lavender. I almost got in my car and drove to the trailhead to try to find him myself. Instead I stayed home and contemplated every scenario: he'd been swept away in an avalanche, broken a leg, gotten sick, fallen in the river, plummeted off a cliff. I briefly considered one where he didn't make it back.

I hoped that he thought about me and everyone else who loved him as he made choices on that trip.

That evening I walked past the kitchen sink, which was filled with dirty dishes. *JT would never let dishes pile up like this*, I thought. *I should really clean this up before he gets home.* I flipped through articles in a *New Yorker* magazine that someone had left at our house. I couldn't make it through more than one page without thinking about JT. Alone at the table, I picked at a bagel, grabbed a couple handfuls of M&Ms, then ate some salmon dip to trick myself into believing I'd eaten a real dinner.

Later that evening I called my friend Jeff, who was involved in the mountain rescue group. "Do you think I should call someone?" I asked.

He knew that "someone" meant the police or the mountain rescue group.

"Oh, man," he said. "I'm sorry."

Jeff knew it was a tough decision. I wondered if he was thinking about all those newspaper articles admonishing 911 calls for twisted ankles or feeling tired.

"It looks like high winds and snow in the mountains. I hate to say it, but we probably couldn't fly too close anyway," he said.

"Listen," I said, "I don't want to make this decision alone." I didn't want to call for help if JT was cozy in his sleeping bag at camp. But I didn't want to wait if he was on the side of that mountain with a life-threatening injury, where every minute mattered.

"I know," he said, "It's a tough call."

We brainstormed options. I simultaneously wanted to honor JT's request that I wait and to know that he was safe. Jeff and I formulated a plan to hike in at first light and assess the conditions ourselves. If we didn't find him at camp, we'd call for help.

I tried going to sleep with the home phone and cell phone beside the bed, ringers turned up as loud as possible. At midnight I was up again, sick with worry.

At 2:00 a.m. the home phone rang.

"Hi, Honey." It was JT's voice.

I flicked the light on beside the bed. "Where are you? Are you okay?"

"Yeah. Sorry it's so late," he said calmly.

"Jesus, I was so scared." My voice got louder than I wanted it to. "I called everyone I could think of and was going to hike in to try to find you. Holy shit, what happened?"

"Everything just took longer," he said. "The snow was soft, which meant post-holing the entire way up. The top was trickier than I remembered. It took a lot longer to climb the final rocky pitch covered in ice. Then it was post-holing all the way down, and then it was dark so everything took longer. You sound worried."

"Of course I'm worried." I gripped the pillow and got teary. "I thought you might have died out there."

"I wasn't *that* late," he said.

"You don't know what it's like on this side. You can't do that to me."

"I'm sorry you were so worried," he said. "Nothing to worry about now. I'll be home in half an hour."

I let the phone drop to the floor, and my whole body released knowing that JT was okay. It didn't make me feel less angry at him, but it occurred to me then that this was part of the fine print regarding the adventure package I'd signed up for. If I was going to accept JT, I'd have to accept this part too.

———

At one in the morning on a remote river bar, with bears all around and a loaded gun by my head, it was easy to imagine a lot of ways to die. Six weeks after JT's delayed return from the climb, I was lying next to him in a tent on a gravel bar near the confluence of the Noatak and

Kelly Rivers in Northwest Alaska, and I was imagining all of them. Every now and then I squeezed JT's hand so hard he flinched.

We were on a twelve-day trip, just the two of us. Assuming we lived through the night, we were going to get married the day after we returned to Anchorage. We'd been calling it the wedding planning protest trip. Determined not to get overwhelmed by the stress that seems to consume couples as wedding day approaches, we'd decided that the solution was to bail. Not just skip town but head to one of the most remote corners of the country, where there would be zero chance of an email or phone call getting through. We'd been apprehensive before the trip because we knew nothing of this country except that it would be only the two of us in a remote place with a lot of bears. We elected to carry a gun, just in case.

That day we'd had a lovely time rafting through the slow meanders of the Noatak River, spent a quiet evening at camp, and then crawled into bed. Alaska is so big, JT remarked, that a person can never fully meet it. We might try our whole lives and only get to know a slim portion of the state. Even the same location will change personalities. I could only imagine being here on the Noatak in the winter when it's fifty below, with howling wind. It would be unrecognizable compared to the mellow float we'd been enjoying.

A couple hours into the night I'd awakened to a sound that prickled the hair on the back of my neck. Something was shuffling over sandy cobbles outside the tent. Why would there be people here in the middle of the night? It didn't sound like the snap of caribou hooves.

I closed my eyes to listen, but the sound was gone. I inched toward the tent door, unzipped it, and peeled back the fabric so I could peek out. Through the Arctic twilight I saw the rumpled fur of a grizzly bear that was clawing at the sand. Then another one walking behind a bush. Then another one, and another. They must be congregating on this gravel bar to feast on salmon.

"JT," I gasped, "they're everywhere. A couple are really close." I huddled toward the center of the tent and strained to listen. "Should we be still, or should we make noise?"

JT slid his hand over to the gun and loaded it.

We sat stiff as wood, barely breathing. Suddenly, *Whoosh!* A bear brushed the guy lines as it ran by the tent, and the tent was shaking. JT grabbed the gun and aimed it—at what?

"What are you doing?" I shrieked. "You can't shoot through the tent!" Adrenaline surged. I realized I'd been holding my breath.

"This isn't good," he said, regaining composure.

"What would prevent a bear from running right over the tent and trampling us?" I wondered out loud. "What if a bear starts biting us through the tent wall, and we're trapped in here?"

"I think we just have to stay here," he said. "They don't seem interested in the tent."

That was when I began to imagine all the ways we might die. We finally dozed off holding onto each other but then woke in a panic at the sound of paws kneading gravel or a bear belly pushing through a bush. Somehow we fell back asleep again.

When morning arrived we looked out to find the beach deserted. I stretched and walked around camp in the morning sun, with bear tracks all around. We inventoried our things: our tent, our raft, and our dry box full of food—all untouched. I considered it an early wedding present, another gift from the bears, and I smiled. I didn't take it for granted that JT and I were each still in one piece and that we'd witnessed bears, unimpeded, doing what they do, doing what they've always done. I smiled because this was our home.

The day we got home Holly flew up from California to officiate our ceremony in the Chugach Mountains. Mom and Dad arrived in time to help with last-minute chores.

"Do you think we have enough heat lamps?" Dad asked after reading the ominous weather forecast.

"It's an Alaska adventure," chirped Mom. "It'll be beautiful no matter what."

Our families were able to drive to the site, and they wore suits and dresses while our Alaska friends arrived in jeans and fleece jackets. Mom and Dad enthusiastically greeted the characters they'd heard so much about: Matt, Butch, Brij, Shelley, Corrina, Becky and her new boyfriend Tony. Mom and Dad got big hugs from everyone, and it made me happy to see them enveloped in our Alaska community.

As our friends and family formed a circle beneath the Twin Peaks, freshly dusted in August snow, JT and I vowed to continue to celebrate life, love, and community here. We vowed to do it as a team and promised each other our love and support. Friends and family stood one at a time to offer inspiration, advice, and reflection. Their words and stories felt like sunshine on bare skin. As JT and I danced and laughed through the afternoon, we felt our toes wriggle a little deeper into this place. Our roots, it seemed, had taken hold.

CARIBOU

The suburban East Coast girl in me never expected to arrive at a point in her life when she was pulling herself uphill through head-high grasses and belly-crawling around rocky outcrops to stalk and perhaps shoot a caribou. One of the strongly held beliefs I'd lugged to Alaska was that it was wrong to hunt. How could anyone kill something as beautiful as a caribou? That's what Mom said to me when I told her I was going to learn to hunt.

"I just can't imagine you . . . *doing* that," she said on the phone, and I wondered if she was right, if I wouldn't get more out of simply observing the caribou and leaving, so that others could do the same.

Maybe it was time to unpack some more of the baggage I'd brought here, though. I felt it also might be time to take some responsibility for my carnivorous diet. With my mother I'd admonished my uncle for hunting but continued to devour steaks and hamburgers. Who could blame me? I had never connected hunting with eating. Growing up on the urban East Coast, I was completely removed from where food came from. As a child it hadn't occurred to me that you could get food from anywhere except a grocery store.

My friends Matt, Becky, and Corrina had contributed freshly caught salmon to our gatherings, and, as years passed, moose, caribou, and sheep roasts had joined salmon at the serving table. At first I'd hesitated to try it, but it hadn't taken me long to develop a taste for wild game. I'd just never imagined I'd be the one pulling the trigger.

When Matt, fellow nature lover and adventurer, started hunting, I began to wonder if I had the gall to try it too. Like me, Matt is from the suburban East Coast, where we tended to associate hunting with rednecks and Bud Light. Matt worked for a nonprofit environmental group, hosted a bluegrass show on public radio, and campaigned for progressive political candidates. Hunting seemed to me like an odd addition to his pursuits. Which made me wonder, was hunting part of the range of experiences I'd hoped to collect here in Alaska?

Despite thirty years of East Coast indoctrination, Alaska changed Matt's opinion. And Matt changed mine.

"Don't you think it's better to know where your food is coming from?" he'd said at dinner one night.

I couldn't argue with that.

When Matt reclined in his chair, a look of playful sparring in his eyes, I could tell he was on the brink of one of his passionate, articulate rambles.

He raised both arms dramatically and addressed me. "A," he said, using a nickname, "You like challenges. I think you should challenge yourself to face more closely something as natural and universal as death."

"Consider the gratitude you would cultivate toward your food," he continued, picking up speed. "Think about eating hormone-free, antibiotic-free, free-ranging meat, and throughout the year being able to share delicious, nourishing food with JT and our friends!"

"And," he said, pausing and running his fingers over his black beard, "I will totally help you do it!" His smile was contagious.

I glanced at JT. He raised his eyebrows and chuckled, "Go for it." He hadn't hunted before either and seemed amused by my interest.

I began to wonder if I was capable of killing something. Could I bring myself to look a living creature in the eye and kill it? It would challenge my own idea of who I was, but I decided I wanted to try. I began to implement a plan to hunt, knowing that I could and would stop if at any moment in the process I felt too uncomfortable. I applied for a number of permits for hunts close to home. A person has to get extraordinarily lucky in the lottery administered by the Alaska Department of Fish and Game to draw a permit for one of the prime hunts close to Anchorage, the preferred hunting grounds of the city's three hundred thousand residents.

Matt called me the moment the names were released: I'd drawn a permit for the Kenai caribou hunt, a challenging but much-sought hunt just two hours from my house.

"A," he said, "I'm reading here that out of the 235 drawing permits issued for this hunt last year, only 17 got an animal."

"That's it?"

"Listen, don't let that discourage you. It's not because the caribou aren't there. They're just hard to get to. But don't worry, *we* can get there!"

We aligned our calendars and circled a long weekend in August.

Matt let me borrow his rifle, a 30.06 he'd bought used from his own hunting mentor, Corrina's boyfriend, Dan. He took me to a shooting range and showed me how to position the butt against my shoulder. I had never held a rifle before, much less felt the powerful recoil. I held it tightly and braced for the kick. Once I knew what to expect, it was manageable. We shot for about an hour. I consistently hit the bull's-eye at a hundred yards. "Nice job, A!" he said. "You're a great shot."

I grinned.

"Now that you know you can do it, don't practice again. Don't wreck your confidence by practicing."

"Okay." I put the rifle down and looked at him. "But how will I know what to aim for when we're out there?" I asked.

"Just look on the internet," he said.

"What?" How was I going to learn about hunting from the internet?

"Search for photos of kill zones on caribou and elk."

"So," I said, "Just look at pictures and visualize where it is on the animal?"

"Yeah. It's funny, but now every time I'm out hiking and see an animal, I zero right in on where I'd shoot it."

I shook my head in mock disbelief. "Who *are* you?" I said, smiling.

On the drive home from the shooting range I asked Matt about butchering.

"I think it's best to learn how to field dress an animal while doing it. We'll work through it together in the field. Once we get home we'll do the same thing with butchering."

"Do I need to bring any other gear?"

"I don't mind if we use all of my stuff, but it would help to have a couple cotton game bags and your own knife. You can pick those up at the butcher supply store in Anchorage. You'll want to bring an old backpack, one you don't mind getting bloody, or one with an external frame."

Matt was grinning. He turned to me. "I love that we're talking about this!"

In mid-August I met Matt after work. He showed me the bone saw and game bags he'd brought and gave me a huge hug. "This is so excitin'!" he shouted in his fake Southern accent. "We goin' huntin'!"

We drove two hours to the community of Hope and camped near the trailhead. The next morning we bushwhacked through overgrown swamp, tightly spaced spruce trees, and fireweed stalks higher than our heads. As we approached tree line, Matt suggested I walk in front and carry the rifle just in case. I pushed through the giant fireweed stalks and emerged into a clearing. I slowly, quietly stepped over blueberry bushes and climbed up toward the first rocky point on the ridge. I nervously glanced around, unsure how things would unfold if I spotted a caribou.

As I came over a little rise, I froze. Something brown was moving across the slope about fifty yards above me. A caribou! But I was too close. If I moved, it would see me and run away. As I slowly knelt down, the caribou looked up and bolted. I ran back toward Matt. "There's a caribou! I don't know if it's big enough. I was so close!"

"That's unbelievable," he said enthusiastically. Neither of us had expected to see one until we were much deeper into the mountains.

We hiked along the ridge until the caribou came into view again.

"It's not huge, but it's plenty big to shoot," said Matt. For hours we stalked that bull up the steep ridge, along grassy knolls and around fins of rock. I felt like a kid clawing over rocks and ducking under bushes. It was fun, completely exhilarating, an adrenaline high, until I got close enough to shoot it and knelt down. I rested the loaded gun in a groove between rock and tundra. Crusty black and mint-colored lichens crinkled under my knees, sunshine warmed my forearms, my hip pressed into a sharp rock, and a wild caribou stood within my sight.

I looked through the scope of the rifle and lined the crosshairs on the caribou. Before I could take a steadying breath, it stepped forward and lay down behind a fin of rock. Through the scope all I could see was the tip of one antler. When it stood, I would be in position to shoot it. Matt shimmied up beside me and crouched behind the rock. We waited. Matt held the caribou in view with his binoculars.

I wondered whether the caribou had sat down for just a moment or whether it was in for a solid afternoon nap.

Next to us a ptarmigan clucked and dashed toward a rock. We looked up. A hawk circled above our heads and dived toward the smaller bird. The ptarmigan scampered beneath a rock and nervously looked for better protection.

"I can't believe they're doing this within ten yards of us, as if they don't know we're here," I whispered to Matt. If the hawk swept down and grabbed the ptarmigan, I was sure we would hear talons closing around downy feathers and crunching fragile bones. The hawk continued to circle, but we didn't have time to watch. The caribou stood, broadside and motionless. A wave of panic washed over me. This was my moment.

My heart raced as I flicked the safety to "fire." I was sure that I was going to shoot that animal and suddenly felt overwhelmingly awful when I knew I couldn't miss.

"I'm going to shoot it," I whispered to Matt. "Should I shoot it? I'm going to shoot it. Oh, my god."

I pressed the butt of the rifle into my shoulder, aimed the crosshairs at the lungs, held my breath, and gently pulled the trigger.

What happened next was incongruous with the quiet of the moment before. I fired the gun, and it felt like thunder in my chest—deep, cracking. The caribou flicked its head twice, as if trying to dislodge a fly from its nose, before staggering backward and down. I was completely out of breath the second I stood and tried to run to it.

It took a couple of minutes to stumble across the rocks and steep slope to kneel beside the fallen animal. I gently placed my hand on his shoulder and felt how warm that caribou was in the August sun, lying in a rock-filled gully, his tongue sliding out of the side of his mouth, light red foam frothing around his lips. Blood sputtered from the hole through his lungs and speckled his gray-brown fur with tiny pricks of bright red blood. I smeared the blood along his neck as I petted him.

"You're so beautiful. I'm sorry I killed you." Probably a dozen times I said that. With the back of my hand I wiped the tears from my cheek.

When I tried to close the caribou's eyes, those liquid glassy eyes, they wouldn't shut, as if he wanted another look around. And when *I* looked around I felt as if something was missing, and I realized that what was missing was the wild creature I'd just killed. I thought that I would almost have enjoyed seeing the caribou alive here more than I would enjoy taking its meat home on my back. But something else told me to endure that feeling, because the power of connecting this strongly with the natural world, and the pride of procuring my own food, might be worth it.

Matt gave me some time alone with the caribou, to make peace with what I had done. He eventually hiked over, rested both of our backpacks on the ground, and admired the shot. "Right through the lungs," he said. "Just like we talked about."

We sat quietly with the caribou, and I said a silent prayer thanking the animal. I had no interest in standing over it with my rifle and posing for a photo. But I took photos of the caribou because to me it was still beautiful and I loved it. Yes, I loved the caribou and was filled with gratitude and respect for it. Never before had I experienced such a connection to a wild creature. I didn't conquer it. I loved it, and I killed it. That's a strange thing to reconcile.

The sun beat down. We were high up on the ridge and out of water. We needed to get to work. Matt showed me how to cut the hide away from the meat, release the stomach cavity, and field-dress it. I recoiled from the stomach cavity and the thought of accidentally piercing that bloated sack, but the more work we did on the animal, the more it felt like a project with a purpose. Having a task to accomplish distracted me from the trauma of having killed a caribou. We put the four quarters in separate game bags and cut off the meat around the ribs and neck. The work took hours. I didn't want to waste any meat. It got hotter. We had no water to wash the drying blood off our hands and arms. We nibbled salty nuts and swallowed dryly.

The meat was heavier than I imagined it would be. Matt, who took the bulk of the load, carried one hundred pounds. A hike that normally takes two hours took us six. We hiked across steep fields of rocks. We balanced on a sharp ridge and teetered under the loads. We bushwhacked through tall grass and climbed over logs. Sometimes we stopped and rested after only ten minutes of walking. It was nearly 11:00 p.m. and dark when we reached the parking lot. When we loaded the game bags into the back of Matt's truck, the meat was still radiating heat, the energy of the animal refusing to die. Exhausted and parched, I climbed into the truck and thought, *I'm glad it wasn't easy. I'm glad killing something wasn't easy.*

On the drive home Matt turned to me and said, "Think of all the caribou Crock-Pot meals you're going to be able to make!"

I thought of the gatherings JT and I frequently hosted and how pleased I was going to feel to provide the centerpiece to meals. I thought about the countless dinners JT and I would share throughout the year, thanks to this caribou.

Just as I was feeling puffed up, Matt chuckled. "A," he said, "You're a killer."

His words felt like an accusation until I turned to see his sincere smile. He was proud of me and, I hope, proud of himself for the hand he played in initiating me.

As Matt drove into the night, a quiet exhaustion settled over me. I stared out the window. A killer? Was that something I wanted to be?

I leaned against the door and rested my head in the palm of my hand. Staring at the empty highway, I contemplated all that had transpired in the day. Did I really just intentionally kill a creature? What was this strange satisfaction I felt?

In a soft voice Matt interrupted the silence and asked if I recalled watching the hawk and ptarmigan. The image was vivid in my mind:

the ptarmigan's nervous scampering, the sunlit wings of the hawk, its eyes following the ptarmigan's every twitch. The hunt, the chase, the dance of predator and prey playing out before us.

Matt looked at me with a crooked smile. "I'm curious," he said. "When we were watching them, which one were you rooting for?"

HOME

They call it an "ice event." It's happening more often with our increasingly erratic Southcentral Alaska winters: periods of extreme cold followed by warm rain and then extreme cold again. It creates a layer of ice an inch—or four inches—thick.

As JT and I walked down our icy driveway, I was trying not to snag my long black velvet skirt with the crampons that I was wearing on my boots. I used the faint beam of light from my headlamp to guide my feet to the edge of the driveway, where there was some crunchy snow on top of the ice. It was so slick that the eighth of a mile took us ten minutes. The wind swirled snow around my feet and blew my hair into tangles. Even after eight years here, I laughed out loud thinking how this scene would amuse my sophisticated brother in San Diego. I could see him cringe and shake his head. "Sis, really?" he'd say. "You can't go out looking like that."

But it was Alaska, and I knew that once we shuffled to the car at the bottom of the driveway and navigated the forty-five-minute drive into Anchorage and negotiated slippery sidewalks to the Alaska Center for the Performing Arts, where the Anchorage Symphony Orchestra would perform, there would be other people who would have worked just as hard to get there. Some would have worked harder, leaving frozen pipes and flooded basements or driving farther, from much more rustic abodes. There would be people in tuxedos and others in Carhartts. And everyone, including me, would fit in perfectly.

We sat comfortably in the balcony as the orchestra began Dimitri Shostakovich's Symphony no. 5 in D Minor, opus 47. The program notes described the famous last movement as a volcanic eruption of musical ideas, which range from grand and powerful to bombastic and theatrical. It warned that the exultant mood did not negate the tragedy at the core of the work.

As I listened to the music I thought of my home and how the valley it is in is often called the Symphony Lake valley for its blue lake with that name. The surrounding symphonic peaks—Harp, Organ, Flute, Hurdy Gurdy, Cantata, Calliope, Triangle, and Concerto—rise thousands of feet from the valley floor, their jagged, snow-covered summits penning in the lake and valley.

I remembered sitting on top of Threebowls a couple of months earlier when the valley was chilly and the mountains looked heavy beneath winter's accumulation of snow. I'd left work early, frustrated by the reality that protecting federally designated wilderness from an onslaught of threats meant that I had entered a battle I could never win. There were thousands of ways to degrade wilderness and no way to create better wilderness. My job was to try to hold the line in a couple of the Alaska national parks, to not let the character and quality of the wilderness diminish.

So I sat on wind-packed snow beneath a rocky outcrop that helped buffer the wind, and I thought about how much I loved that ridge, the level ramp that connects the high points behind our house. I could make out our house almost twenty-five hundred feet below and could vaguely see when a car drove up the driveway, although I was too far away to see a person. I dug my heels into the snow and positioned my bottom on my backpack so I wouldn't get cold. The wind crinkled the hood of my down jacket. When I shifted my weight, the snow crunched. Otherwise there was only that hollow sound that for me epitomizes being by myself outside in winter. It was utterly quiet but not silent: the symphonic peaks seemed to emit a vibration that evoked a feeling of rapture within me, beauty that commanded a pause.

That day I'd carried home worries over legislators who wanted to build roads through wilderness areas, the state's desire to keep shooting wolves, my well-meaning colleagues who wanted to land helicopters and install more scientific instruments in the wilderness, and upper-level managers who were afraid of the political ramifications of curtailing a disruptive amount of recreational snowmobiling. That sound of stillness was about the only thing that made my mind feel lighter, however briefly, and simply consider where I was. Worries about work dissolved into the snow and the light. All that mattered was the soft pink glow on the snowy chutes, the wild empty space at my toes.

I glanced toward the high point to my right, the rocky knoll we now called Proposal Point. I imagined a younger version of JT looking up at that point on the ridge and figuring it would be a good and proper place to propose to his future wife.

From Proposal Point, the ridge wraps around the tops of the bowls and tapers into a steep ramp that returns to our house. We can walk the loop in two hours if we keep a good pace. On that ridge we've seen grizzly bears, Dall sheep, and wolverines. In the gully we've watched bull moose with enormous racks bedded down on the hillside. We can tell you where the best blueberry patches are, which lines to ski to avoid the rocks early in the season, and where the natural springs start. From the top of Threebowls I scanned every boulder, dip, and prominent point and recalled a part of my life in each.

I recalled Archimedes, who had loved Threebowls as much as JT and I did. I remembered how he would press his nose to moose tracks and drink from a spring and chase ptarmigan he had no chance of catching. JT spent more time with that goofy 110-pound dog than with anyone else. For six years the two had spent nearly every summer day climbing Chugach peaks and nearly every winter weekend chasing each other up and down backcountry ski slopes. Some days when I'd ask JT about one of his long climbs and add, with a creased brow, "Did you go alone?" He would respond, "No, Arc went with me."

Arc began to die not long after JT and I got married. After he became constipated and lost his appetite, a veterinarian removed a cancerous growth in his colon. JT stayed with Arc all night at the vet, and then, bleary-eyed, brought him home and carried him from the truck to our living room floor. Over the next couple days, JT lovingly stroked Arc's knobby head as he went from constipated to incontinent. We lived with shit all over the house for a while, despite how many sheets we put down to cover the floor, before banishing Arc to the patio, where magpies tormented him and stole the kibbles that he didn't care to eat.

The cancer came back, and the vet said his days were numbered. JT cooked him hamburgers and salmon and recounted the story about falling in love with him at the pound. "You were just a little hound puppy on the side of the road in Palmer," he'd begin. A young man on a motorcycle had spotted an abandoned Arc sitting beside a pile of dog food, stopped, and scooped him into his lap. He'd balanced the puppy, half on his lap and half on the handlebars, while he drove all the way back to Anchorage. The man couldn't keep the pup, so he reluctantly brought him to the pound, where JT discovered him. Years later a mutual friend saw a photo of Arc on that guy's refrigerator and put the pieces together.

JT called the vet when Arc could no longer eat. Arc's eyes, once bright and mischievous, were glazed over. I came home from work to find JT on the living room floor, snuggled up against Arc. He was paging through a photo album of a trip they'd done together. JT held each photo up to Arc's face so that he could see it and then reminded Arc which trip it was from.

Arc liked to drink from a trickle of a creek next to our house. There, on a patch of grass beside the creek where wildflowers grew, the vet administered the pink fluid that would kill him. It was late fall. JT loaded Arc's limp, heavy body onto a sled and pulled him up through the bushes behind our house to the grave he'd dug a month earlier, before the ground had frozen. A car-sized boulder, speckled black, gray, and white, marks the spot.

A month later, after a wolverine dug him up and licked his bones, we buried him again.

———

While sitting on that snowy ridge, it was impossible to distinguish the features of the landscape from the facets of my life. It had been just uphill from that rock, on a flat patch of open ground, that we'd invited our friends to celebrate JT's fortieth birthday. Matt, Todd, Corrina, Tony, and Becky had hauled sleds filled with beer and children through rotten spring snow to a patch of dry ground. Others had post-holed through thigh-deep snow carrying charcoal grills and moose sausages. Becky and I had snowshoed up one of the slopes and marked a giant red "40" with Kool-Aid on the side of the mountain.

JT had been flattered that so many people came, but he'd also seemed quieter than usual.

"You doing okay?"

"Yeah. I guess I'm just not that excited about turning forty."

"A lot of people seem to peak in their forties," I'd offered. "You know, athletically and career-wise."

"Sometimes I wonder what I'm doing. I mean, I don't feel like I'm working toward making a difference in the world."

I'd looked at him sideways.

"I wonder if being a teacher is really something I can do for another ten or fifteen years. I'm still two dozen peaks shy of climbing all 122 Chugach peaks." He'd looked down then. "If I ever have children, I'm going to be too old to do anything with them."

I had listened to him but wasn't quite sure what he was talking about. He seemed to have a pretty great life.

Just then our neighbor Brad, having skied down Threebowls, had skidded to a stop in the melting snow beside the party. JT had given him a hug and handed him a beer.

Todd's daughter had tugged on JT's pant leg. "Will you juggle?" she'd asked.

"Yeah I will!" he'd said, grabbing the closest three objects. His friends had laughed and egged him on, successfully distracting him from the onset of his midlife crisis.

———

Each month of the year JT and I go to the top of the ridge. Some months it's dry and sunny, and other times we snowshoe or ski with skins. Sometimes the snow is so packed and icy that we need crampons to make it to the top. Other times the snow is so unstable and the fear of avalanche so high that we follow the ridge and don't go near the hollow bowls. Massive avalanches rip down Threebowls every year. At times they've buried dogs. Once, one claimed a neighbor.

I remember one afternoon, in the middle of winter, standing on top and wondering if the mountain would let me return home safely. I was in a shallow trough surrounded by an arc of packed snow, taking off my climbing skins and clicking my ski boots into the bindings. Beside me, snow blew sideways around a boulder. Todd and I put on our warmest down jackets and ski goggles and swapped soaked gloves for big mitts. We checked to make sure our avalanche beacons were switched on. As Todd zipped up his hooded jacket he said, "Prepare for burial, just in case the snowpack isn't as stable as we hope."

He could not have said anything that would have made me feel more sick to my stomach. Scraping metal ski edges into the crust, I skidded over the cornice. I angled down, carved a wide arc, and stopped. Deep snow in the gut of the run had slowed my turn. The chute was plenty steep to slide, and if it slid I'd have nowhere to go. I looked uphill and thought, *There's a lot of snow above me.* That sick feeling swirled again. I realized with every turn that I was anticipating the feeling of snow giving out beneath my skis and washing me down the mountain in a tremendous violent wave.

Only the top few inches of snow are sloughing off, I reassured myself. I sliced the skis again and again through the powder, feeling like a child taking something without asking, then running away. Below, the South Fork Valley glowed in pink afternoon light. Every turn I safely completed, I was thankful the mountain let me have this moment. I bargained with the universe: if you let me have just a few more turns I promise I'll never ski on steep, unstable slopes ever again.

I say that I go to the top of Threebowls to look at the view of Denali to the north or the rugged peaks above the Eagle River Valley to the east or across to Temptation Peak and Cook Inlet to the west. The truth is that most of the time my excursions are more about looking inside myself than looking out at the views.

In the spring when the days are longer I rush home from work, and August follows me as I skin up as fast as I can. We sit on top of Threebowls about eight feet apart and face the same direction. I place my soaked gloves beside me to dry in the sun. I jam my thermos into the snow and curl bare fingers around a cup of hot tea. The sun glistens off August's back, and his coat shines orange with golden highlights. He squints at something down in the snowy bowl, perceiving movement among the avalanche rubble. I look at the same chute and see nothing. Sun on our faces, we both keep squinting. And it occurs to me that this is a lot better than a lot of things I could be doing.

When my tea is gone and my hands are getting cold, I clamp my ski boots into my skis. It is quiet all around. I stand there for a moment feeling the cold stiffen my cheeks and seep through my puffy jacket. My damp gloves start to crust with ice. I point my skis toward our little house below and glide into the bowl. Snow flies up over my knees. August chases me down, running a straight line through the center of my turns. I carve turns through the pink light until I am out of breath. I stop halfway down the mountain to rest and revel in the peace of my backyard, the joy of coming home.

I'd been thinking about the concept of home a lot and wondering what it means and whether I'd found it. It seems prudent to evaluate your choice of home every so often. I wonder how much it has to do with location or family or community or work or state of mind. I call this place home and mean it. I wonder if I always will.

We had been talking about this over dinner with Becky and Tony. They live in a cabin the next valley over. Their cabin has two rooms and no running water and a backyard that they love.

We sat cross-legged on the floor with deep plates piled with food the four of us had fished, hunted, and gathered: salmon fillets, caribou steaks, sautéed morels, and blueberry pie. Becky threw her waist-long braid over her shoulder and caught Tony's eye. They smiled and clinked their forks together—a gesture of gratitude for the food and acknowledgment of sharing it.

"We've been wondering if there's somewhere else, farther from Anchorage, where we could live closer to the land," Tony said.

"How about the South Fork?" JT joked. We'd kept trying to talk them into moving closer to us.

Becky laughed and then cleared her throat, "Actually we've been looking at land. McCarthy, Chickaloon, Seldovia, Haines, we're kind of all over the map right now."

I couldn't swallow my sip of wine at the thought of two of our closest friends leaving.

Tony wiped a swatch of blond hair from his eyes and said earnestly, "I've been reading a bunch about how to build a yurt."

I could tell from the light in his eyes that this wasn't a fleeting fantasy. Tony and Becky weren't afraid to take on complicated projects, do research, and work hard to see them through. I thought, *This is actually something they will do.* This came on the heels of Shelley having told me that she too had made the tough decision to leave. Soon she would depart for Washington to begin graduate school and live closer to her family. I thought about living in Eagle River without Tony, Becky, and Shelley and how noticeable the void in our community would be. They came to our house more than anyone else, and I loved sharing meals, music, and deep conversation with them. We called them almost every weekend to see what they were doing.

I was somewhat surprised that Tony and Becky would choose place over friends. If they moved they would have to start over in building a community. But they itched to live a different lifestyle, one much less reliant on cars, one that moved at a slower pace, one imbued with greater intention. We all agreed that home is a place where we can feel fulfilled. Despite the beauty of this place and our rock-solid community here, their desire to live closer to the land was making them wonder if a place more remote than Eagle River would feel more like home. I had to remind myself not to take their desire to move personally. Not everyone was as fortunate as I was to have found an ideal location and community in the same place.

I smiled at their excitement, but it felt like the smiles my parents showed me when I left for college.

Before dinner we'd climbed the hill behind their house, *their* back-yard. Every direction was frozen white: snow and ice swirled and streaked by wind, current, and topography. A mix of water, ice, and mud ebbed and flowed in the Knik River. An ice-choked tide surged, then retreated, stretching out lines of muddy ice like Silly Putty. Streaked with rivulets of ice, the river itself resembled a glacier with distinct lateral moraines. The inlet too was patterned with swirls of ice that turned pink in the evening glow.

Frost covered all the houses we could see, and all the frozenness in every direction pressed on us a grave sense of vastness and exposure. For about two hours, the extreme beauty of sunset near the darkest day of the year glowed on the horizon to the northwest. While cold darkness swallowed the valleys behind us, a band of pinkish-orange backlit the western part of the Alaska Range and the volcanoes across Cook Inlet.

During this season it is easy to spiral into a cold sadness like the swirled ice in Cook Inlet. Sometimes, when the sun rises at 11:00 a.m. and sets at 3:00 p.m. and is never bright or warm, it can take tremendous effort to be moved into happiness. But up there in Tony and Becky's backyard, in these mountains that are our home, it was hard to believe that sadness could coexist with such beauty.

———

I sat with a concert hall full of people willing to brave one of Anchorage's worst ice storms to listen to music, willing to risk falls and freezing in order to appreciate something beautiful. At the powerful end of the Shostakovich symphony and the beating of drums, I gripped JT's arm and felt adrenaline tingle through my body. This is what I've found in Alaska: rare moments of beauty and community and inspiration tangled up in moments of suffering. Maybe home is the place where both are welcome without judgment. It is where we learn to sit with joy and sadness, finding peace between the extremes, like the pause between each breath.

DESPERATION

It was late August when Becky and I climbed out of the floatplane and piled our backpacks on the slim gravel shore of Feniak Lake. Despite the sun, the air was chilly, so we put on down jackets and fleece hats. I caught Becky's attention and raised my eyes in the direction of the fresh snow on the peaks behind the lake. She pointed to something moving in the distance. A small group of caribou pranced across the plains, heads high, as if there were no tussocks at all.

Alaska adventurer Roman Dial once calculated the distance from roads, airstrips, and villages and then marked a point on the map in the western Brooks Range that he deemed the most remote spot in the United States. We were about twenty miles from that spot. Ever since Tony, Becky, JT, and I had boated and hiked through the Arctic National Wildlife Refuge a couple of years earlier, we had wanted to return to the Arctic. JT and Tony had made a number of big climbs and packraft trips, and now their teaching jobs had them back in the classroom. Becky and I had not been able to let go of the Arctic, and so we'd planned a trip without them.

We stood on the shore and watched the plane lift off the water. It made a wide arc over the lake, swept across the red and gold expanse of tundra, angled west toward Kotzebue, and quickly faded out of sight, leaving us in the wide-open Arctic silence.

Becky and I looked at each other and grinned. We had eight days to walk through the country on a meandering route to Desperation Lake. In front of us, Feniak Lake looked like a giant glassy eye on the big smooth plains. I couldn't help but stare into it.

"Feniak Lake looks lovely," said Becky.

"Want to spend the afternoon walking around it?"

As always, I found the balance tricky. Not the uneven footing but rather balancing my desire to quietly immerse myself in my surroundings with the desire for meaningful connection with a companion. Navigating down the middle is like tap dancing through a field of tussocks.

We started out quietly, tracing the lakeshore, weaving through willows and bogs. We discovered bird tracks, found a big feather, and delighted at the squish of tundra under our feet. We got accustomed to the quiet sound of our breathing and the scratch of willow branches across our hiking pants.

Eventually I spoke up. "Do you have any moving updates?"

Becky glanced in my direction. "We're still collecting and peeling birch and spruce for the roof of the yurt," she said, "but we're not totally sure where we're going to put it. We found land in McCarthy, but we haven't closed on it yet."

We shuffled along side by side.

"We'll come back and visit as much as we can," she said at last.

I glanced behind us to gauge how far we'd come from our drop-off point.

A bit later I engaged Becky again. "So, have you and Tony talked any more about getting married?" It seemed unnecessary to tell her how much JT and I and all of our friends keep hoping they'll get married.

"A little," she said in a tone that seemed more diplomatic than hopeful. "He still isn't sure about the idea of marriage."

"Oh, Bec," I sighed. "I guess people figure these things out in their own way. I'm sorry."

"Yeah," she said and looked at her feet.

We walked in silence for a while until Becky shouted, "Look at that! It's—a fox on that hill. With a kit. With another. Oh my, they keep coming! How cute!" The kits scuttled and rolled over one another. Beside the den the adult squared her white chest toward us. She swiveled her nose toward the kits, then followed us with steady black eyes. I immediately thought of JT, that he'd love to see this, but thinking of him left me remembering the tension in our exchange before I left for this trip.

Becky broke my thought and asked about my parents, and from there our conversation wandered like fox tracks around the lake, delving into dreams, fears, friends, and the natural world around us.

After a few hours, we were back where we started, hungry for dinner. Becky took the aluminum pot to the lake to collect water, and I began assembling the stove. I held the stove in one hand and the fuel bottle in the other and in an instant of horror saw that there were no other pieces in the stove bag. The fuel pump was missing. My throat tightened. We were in one of the most remote places on Earth, the temperatures were near freezing, the airplane wouldn't return for eight days, and we had no stove.

"Becky," I said, cringing. "I have some not-so-great news."

"What's that?" She set the full pot of water beside the stove.

"The stove doesn't work," I said, showing her the fuel bottle. "It's plugged with a plastic cap. I forgot to check the stove bag before we left. We're missing the part that attaches the stove to the fuel bottle."

Her face turned serious for about a half second. Then she said "Well, that's great! I love making fires! Why is it the guys always make the fires? Now *we* get to!"

This is why I continue to ask Becky to do trips with me. We walked over to the lake and started collecting sticks that had washed to shore.

All of a sudden I was acutely aware that there are no trees in this part of the Arctic. Finding firewood seemed like it was going to be a challenge, but I focused on Becky's enthusiasm for fire-building and continued collecting small bleached willow twigs.

We made a teepee out of the tiniest twigs. Becky tore a small slice of paper from her journal and wedged it into the sticks. The little fire caught, and we added larger sticks until our fire was about a foot and a half across. Then we set our pot right in the middle of it. Flames lapped at the pot, and we added twigs until the water boiled to rehydrate our ham-and-mushroom risotto.

As we finished the last bites of dinner I thought about the week ahead of us. "It's going to be more difficult to find wood once we leave the lake."

"Yeah," she said, "Maybe we should take some with us."

"I have a garbage bag we could use. I brought it as an extra waterproof liner for my backpack, but this seems like a higher calling."

"I have the same thing," she said.

After dinner we filled the bags with as much wood as we could fit in them, and it appeared to be an ample amount. Still, it made me nervous to leave the wood supply at Feniak Lake.

The following day we strapped the bags of wood to our packs and set off toward the mountains. We heard not a single engine and saw no sign of other campers. It was just us in the wet fall tundra, crumbling rocky mountains, gravelly rivers, squishy tussocks, small dark blueberries, rainbows, and wind, with cold fingers, wind-whipped hair, and, in the evening, our cozy tent with a vestibule stuffed with wet shoes and two garbage bags bulging with twigs.

Our first evening away from the lake we discovered little twigs on the tundra, white as bleached antlers, and other woody debris scattered around creek deltas. We had no problem making tea and cooking meals with our pot set in the middle of our hungry little fire. But our route was about to take us up over the mountains into a rocky area devoid of vegetation. Carrying bags of sticks had seemed silly at first, but as Becky and I ascended the next day toward a broad rocky saddle, I was glad to be carrying them.

It was one of those unhurried days you hope for on a backcountry trip: fairly easy walking, no bugs, and plenty of time to bask. We meandered toward the saddle, admired a flower here and there, wondered where the caribou were, and twirled around from time to time to take it all in. But close to the saddle the sun suddenly disappeared. The temperature dropped, the wind picked up, and the sky darkened.

Becky shouted over the wind, something about needing to put on another jacket. I cinched my hood and looked behind us. A big, fast-moving storm was about to overtake us.

We quickly found the only spot in sight that wasn't covered by rocks, and we pitched the tent. My fingers were cold. The wind lashed us in waves that got stronger and stronger. I remembered standing outside my house in an 85 mph windstorm just to see what it was like, and this storm felt just as powerful. A gust thundered downslope toward us. "Watch out," I shouted to Becky right before it knocked us sideways. We stumbled and touched the ground with our hands to avoid falling.

Under the dark sky our red tent was a blister on the rocky moonscape. It didn't look terribly inviting, but one at a time we ducked in and sat, and then we recalibrated. Although it was loud in the tent, there was no wind slamming into our eyes. It felt like a time-out, a place to think. Without speaking we both knew that we would wait out the storm inside it.

Another deep rumble of wind built to a deafening crescendo. I looked at the tent wall and braced for impact. The tent wall bent inward, and I shouted at Becky, "What sort of tests do you think the Hilleberg company does to see if a tent can withstand 85 mph gusts?"

"I hope some really good ones!" she shouted back, leaning into the side of the tent as another big gust flexed the tent wall. Soon the wind was flinging rain at the tent in loud splats.

Later in the evening, when it seemed like the wind was easing, we got out of the tent. A small lake, bright turquoise despite the clouds and rain, with whitecaps on its surface, lay nearby. We filled our water bottles in the lake, but drinking cold water in the cold storm wasn't too appealing.

"What about getting a fire going?" I suggested.

Becky found a slight depression in the field of rocks and built a wind block. We crouched behind it and took turns adding sticks and positioning our bodies to buffer the gusts. We burned through one of our bags of sticks, and the smoky fire generated enough heat to cook a pot of rice and beans.

Throughout the night, rain and wind hammered the tent so violently I wasn't sure the tent material would hold. I ran through scenarios of the tent ripping to shreds and thought to myself, *what would we do?*

As I lay there listening, I came back to the conversation I'd had with JT.

We'd been eating dinner when he'd said casually, "So, have you thought about having kids?"

"Really?" I'd said, scrunching my face. "I thought we weren't going to have kids."

"We never decided that," he'd quipped. "When we got married we both said we weren't sure."

"That's weird because I remember feeling sure, and I remember you saying you didn't think you wanted to." I'd suddenly felt dizzy. "Are you asking because you want to have kids now?"

"Well, maybe. I just need to know if you're open to it." He'd wiped his mouth with a cloth napkin. "I *hope* you're open to it."

My mind replayed the scene over and over until I exhausted myself with worry and succumbed to sleep.

In the morning Becky and I woke to a sideways downpour, and we didn't even think about making a fire. We estimated the temperature to be in the mid-thirties, with an unknown but painfully cold windchill. Two inches of water had pooled on the ground beneath the vestibule, but since it was the only open patch in a field of rock, there was nowhere to move. We shifted our pile of sticks to the highest ground inside the vestibule and covered it with empty bags. We stayed in the tent until noon, not drinking any water—to avoid having to go outside to pee.

That afternoon we lay on our backs, alternating between reading and napping.

"Hey, Bec," I said, "Do you think there's any way we could make a break for it? I bet the weather would be better if we got out of the pass."

"It *might* work," she said hesitantly. "How do you think our sleeping bags would do?"

Since our garbage bags had been pierced with sticks, we only had nylon stuff sacks to protect our sleeping bags.

"What if we conduct a test?" I asked. "We could walk around for a little while with a bandana in a stuff sack in our backpack and see what happens."

"I have one right here," she said, sitting up. "Let's do it!"

Anything to get out of the tent.

We put her bandana in a stuff sack inside a garbage bag inside her backpack, wiggled into rain gear, and set off hiking up a side valley in driving rain. We hopped and teetered across lichen-covered rocks while wispy clouds swirled over the dark peaks. I paused to look around. Using my hands to shield my eyes from the rain, I saw through a curtain of clouds and mist a caribou clipping past the lake as if she were in a big hurry. I looked around for others, but she and her two little ones were alone. The thought of her shepherding them across the whole dang Arctic nearly broke my heart.

Despite all our waterproof gear, we returned to camp soaking wet. Sideways rain had seeped under our rubber hoods and elastic wristbands. The "water resistant" material in our backpacks and stuff sacks was no match for the storm. Becky's bandana was drenched. The holey garbage bags, which were our only real hope for keeping something dry, were useless. We would not be able to safely transport our sleeping bags and down jackets to a new camp. If they got wet, we would freeze.

That evening Becky and I sat in the tent hunched over our food. I ate sausage and cheese for dinner and licked the grease and spices off my cold fingers. I didn't think about JT and what to do about having children. I didn't wonder what the future held for us. I only thought about filling my belly and keeping my sleeping bag dry.

The following day was identical, although sometimes it sleeted instead of rained. Becky and I huddled in the tent, and when we heard the growl of a big gust coming, we held our breath and braced our arms in front of our faces as the wind smashed in the tent walls. I shook my head after one such gust. It seemed like a miracle that the tent was still standing after thirty hours of blasting wind and rain.

The weather had become a sentient being with a malicious personality. I stifled an urge to shout, "Why are you doing this to us? We don't deserve this!" But the wind and sleet wouldn't listen, and the mountains didn't protect us. They didn't care at all.

The next day was the same again, except that we were out of food that didn't need to be cooked. If we'd had a working stove, we could have sipped hot drinks all day, looked forward to bubbling bowls of stew, heated the tent, and dried our clothes in the vestibule. Instead we lay next to each other for hours without speaking.

Finally Becky broke the silence. "So, how are you and JT doing?" "We're okay," I told her. "Not great."

I took a deep breath and decided to tell her. "He started talking about having children, and you know I've never wanted kids. I didn't think he wanted kids either, but now he does. He seems like a different person."

"Really? I had no idea." She took a few breaths and then said steadily, "And why don't you want kids?"

"So many reasons." I launched into it. "I'm afraid I won't be able to do any of the things I love. I mean, I couldn't be on this trip with you if I had a baby, right? I couldn't keep traveling internationally, at least not in the way I'm used to. I'm afraid JT and I would never do anything together. You know how I need my space. I can't imagine someone needing me and being attached to me all the time. Plus, I wouldn't know what to do with a baby. I don't think I even *like* kids!"

"Those all seem like good reasons," Becky said as she rolled over in her sleeping bag. "Do you ever think about the benefits of having kids?"

I stared at the ceiling. "It's really hard for me to see any, but, yeah, part of me wonders why nearly everyone does it. I don't want to miss out on a part of life that's really meaningful, if it is."

"So what are you going to do?"

"I don't know! I felt so angry when he brought it up. I felt like he betrayed me, changing his mind like that. Then sometimes I wonder, would I really hate it, or would it be okay?"

This was the first time I'd shared any of this. For a minute it felt like I'd just listened to someone else rant, someone desperate and afraid. I felt my ears heating.

What would I do if the foundation I so carefully constructed were to fall apart? In the past I'd relied on intuition to make decisions: that the West held my future, that I should take the ranger job in Alaska, that I would be happy marrying JT. Feeling confused by my lack of intuition, I inhaled deeply and then sighed.

I left the tent to pee and to dunk a water jug in an icy puddle. When I returned to the tent, my cold wet fingers fumbled with the tent zipper, and it took an hour to warm up again in my sleeping bag. My crisis over having children haunted me, but I didn't bring it up again. It felt good to have gotten it out there, to have Becky know.

———

Throughout the evening we shifted from side to side. Our hips ached from lying down for most of the preceding fifty-four hours.

Becky closed her book on her chest and stared at the tent ceiling. "How great would that mac and cheese dinner be right now?" she said soberly.

I rolled over onto my side so that I was facing her, and I cinched the opening of my sleeping bag around my neck so the warmish air wouldn't leak out.

"It would be pretty great," I said. "I would do about anything for even one bite of something hot."

Becky sat up and crouched over. The tent wasn't quite tall enough for sitting fully upright. She pushed a wisp of damp hair back under her wool hat.

"What if we tried," she said. Determination had replaced her cheerful optimism, and she was ready to spring to action.

"Okay," I said. "If you really want to do this, we can try."

Becky laid out the plan. "I'll leave the tent first," she said. "I'll fit as many sticks as I can under my coat, and I'll reinforce the rock wall."

"How long do you think I should wait?" I asked.

"Give me a three-minute head start. I'll fix the wall and dig out a depression. It seems like the wind's coming from two directions, so if the fire isn't down low it'll get blown away."

I tried to visualize each move I'd make when I left the tent. It would be brutal the second I stepped out. "I'll bring the pot and water bottle and take another load of sticks under my jacket," I said. "I'll see you at the wall."

After Becky left the tent, I waited and then took the pot and second bundle of wood and hugged them to my chest as I balanced on slippery rocks and made it the fifty yards to the rock wall. Clouds enveloped most of the mountains and wind kicked up a spray across the lake. By the time I arrived, Becky had placed a good amount of fuel on the pile of twigs and gotten a couple to light, but they were only smoking—there was no flame. I squatted in the smoke, two feet from the fire pit, clutching a bundle of damp twigs. Unable to see, I groped for another precious semidry stick to place on the fire. Even doused in white gas they were barely burning.

Becky's gloves were soaked and missing the thumb and forefingers, but she managed to grasp tiny pieces of willow twigs and place them like a teepee in the fire pit. Again she poured fuel over the twigs. Then came the hard part. With frozen fingers we each tried to flick the lighter but couldn't spin the metal wheel well enough to get a flame. It sparked but didn't light. A huge gust of wind blew, and Becky and I put our hands on the rocks to keep them from falling in. I looked up to see a wall of rain blowing toward us. We ducked down until it passed. Becky tried the lighter again, and finally a spark ignited the pile. We set the pot of water right in the middle of the flame as another wall of rain slammed into our faces. We scooted as close as possible to the fire and huddled over it, squinting into an icy, sideways downpour. I sat on a sharp rock, but my legs were too cold and cramped to move. All of my five layers were wet.

Without speaking or looking at each other, we knew it was a race. The twigs burned almost instantly. They were light as air and didn't hold fire, so we had to keep adding them quickly or the fire would go out. And quickly we were behind.

Another big gust of wind and sheet of rain blew over us. We ducked and tried to shield the fire, but it went out. Becky scrambled to her knees and elbows, pressed her cheek into the wet, sooty rock and blew. A cloud of ashes billowed back at her. She took another breath and blew again. This time the fire came back. We added one twig at a time to this one-square-foot patch of Arctic that had all of our attention.

I ached to feel warmth from the fire, so I scooted closer until my knees were inches from the weak flames and my face was in the smoke. My eyes burned and watered, and I assessed the pile of twigs that remained. The pile was shrinking fast, and the water looked barely warm. The rain turned to hail, and the icy bullets pounded us. I ducked to protect my face while hail stung my ears, forehead, arms, and knees. Without looking up, we searched the ground blindly with cold fingers for another twig. The fire was dying.

Becky squinted into the hail, repositioned twigs, and blew. All we needed were two cups of hot water for semicooked pasta. The fire ignited again.

My hands were shaking too much to place twigs on the fire so I scooped them and handed them to Becky. Tears from smoke and icy wind streamed down my cheeks, though I may as well have been crying for how badly I wanted a cup of hot water.

We were out of wood. Becky held the last twig, and, instead of putting it on the fire, she used it to flip the lid off the pot. We peered in and saw little pearls of air rising from the bottom. It would do.

In the tent, we spooned partly cooked (but warm) mac and cheese into our mouths.

"I don't think I've ever worked so hard for such a mediocre meal that tasted so good," I told Becky, and she smiled.

The following day the winds calmed, and we made a break, scurrying out of the saddle, down from the rocks, and into the red and yellow tundra. A beautiful creek there and slanting light on never-ending ridges made it seem like a new world. It also made me wonder whether the storm brimming inside myself would end this way—whether I would crawl out, wet and humbled. Storms end eventually, but people don't always emerge from them unscathed. Out of nowhere I told Becky that I was afraid.

"For me and JT," I added.

"I think there's a reason you two are together," she said reassuringly. "I think you'll find each other again. As long as you come back to what brought you together."

I wanted to believe her.

I peeled off my wet gloves, revealing pale, clammy, wrinkled hands. But the sun erased those signs of struggle and burned color back into my palms, just as it dried the bear trails and made the caribou ruts easier to walk on.

In the distance, a half-day's walk ahead, were the wood-littered shores of Desperation Lake. I fixed my gaze on the horizon and relaxed into my stride. My fingers tingled with warmth, and a thought crept in as gently as a soft breeze caressing cotton grass: sure as the sun, a dark storm will cloud the skies again, and I will hold onto the hope of emerging intact on the other side.

BEACH WALK

The following summer I was stranded on Nunaluk Spit with JT and a group of our friends, waiting for a bush plane that was stuck in fog-covered Inuvik, the nearest village, about an hour flight away. It was early morning on this sliver of gravel and driftwood that separates the Canadian Northwest Territories from the Arctic Ocean. We had been camped here for two days after spending two weeks rafting the Firth River, which spills out of the Brooks Range into an expansive delta and empties into the ocean.

Still groggy with sleep, I slipped out of the tent before JT woke up, and I propped myself against a log. The plain of water extending from the beach, silver as mercury, was so vast that it seemed to muffle the rush of waves that fringed it. The sun was at eye level, and I was squinting right into it. The skinny spit extended to my right and left as far as I could see. Big logs bleached white from the Arctic sun looked like pick-up sticks all over the beach, and I contemplated the force of wind and water that carried them onto the spit. A seal head popped out of the water and then quickly ducked back under and was gone.

Behind me I heard someone unzip a tent door, and I hoped it wasn't JT. I froze and listened. It was quiet again. It must have been one of our friends peeking out to check the weather. I wondered how much longer I could avoid JT.

For the past few months, and more profoundly during the preceding two weeks, I'd found myself engaging JT on logistical matters and otherwise keeping my distance. Maybe if we didn't talk about having kids for long enough he'd move on.

The day before he'd asked if I was ready for breakfast. "I'll bring our food over to the stove," I said and busied myself with preparing food.

Later I asked, "Can we strap the day bags behind you today?" Then I turned around to schlep a few dry bags to the boat.

When there was too much silence I asked, "How far do you think we'll get today?"

I didn't ask what was on his mind. I didn't share my hopes for the future.

Sitting in the early morning calm, I yearned for a time when life felt less complicated. There isn't a time when I am at a beach in the morning that I don't think about the early morning walks with my dad when I was a little girl at the Jersey Shore. He would wake me up at 5:00 a.m., sometimes earlier, and I'd force myself up even though I wasn't ready to be awake. I'd slide my feet into sandals that were cold and sandy from the previous day's post-beach shower. We'd grab a sweatshirt and windbreaker and drive a few blocks to the beach. Even at nine years old, I recognized what a good thing it is to wake up on a beach walk.

Dad and I would walk from the street onto a thin sandy path. We knew we were almost there when the sand got deeper and the wind tangled my hair and the air tasted like seaweed and salt. I would run down the dune to the open beach as the ocean spray made my sweatshirt feel damp. Dad and I would comb the sandy beach, collecting pretty stones, crab shells, and little white and pink conchs. When I was older, in high school, we simply walked and felt invigorated by cool ocean air. Sometimes we would walk side by side, and sometimes we combed our own swatch of sand. Sometimes we talked, but most of the time, I remember, I heard only crashing waves and the cry of seagulls. As a wave slid up the ramp of sand, I would wonder where the water had been, circling the globe, swirling to unfathomably cold depths where creatures we don't even know about glide through the dark, and cycling back to the surface, pulling along horseshoe crabs and gobs of seaweed, and suspending gulls and pelicans. Occasionally one or two other early morning walkers canvassed the beach, but mostly it was just us, with all the water in the world at our feet.

In a few hours the beach would be as packed as a parking lot before Christmas. Crowds would tile the shore with brightly colored towels, umbrellas, lounge chairs, plastic buckets, boogie boards, and sand castles. It would smell of hot sandwiches and suntan lotion. But at five in the morning it was only our footprints in the sand.

The real magic took place when an arc of orange sun lifted above the horizon like a blazing sea monster rising from the ocean. As it slowly rose, the water changed from silver to a tangerine sizzle of broken waves sliding across wet sand. Dad and I would stop walking and face it, letting the glow warm us. When I was nine, watching the sun come up felt like witnessing a big secret, and at sixteen it still moved me.

Recalling those mornings, I wondered if I ought to talk with my parents about the difficulty I was having with JT, but then, embarrassed to admit to them that I was having trouble, I quickly dismissed that thought. In addition to my not wanting them to worry, it also vaguely felt like I'd done something wrong, that I should have verified before getting married that JT didn't want children—or that as a woman I should naturally *want* to have children. Also, I'd fledged. It was no longer appropriate or possible for them to help me with everything.

In front of me a sandpiper skimmed the water, and my thoughts shifted again to those summer mornings with my dad. We would watch until the sun turned from molten orange to simply bright. We'd take off our jackets, gather our seashells if we had collected any, and head back to the beach entrance. Walking along the narrow sandy path through the dune grass, Dad would suggest we bring back doughnuts for everyone. He'd say it casually as if he were indifferent. My enthusiastic endorsement put the plan in motion. And we both knew the truth—none of our slumbering family and friends at the shore house cared if we brought back doughnuts or not. Dad and I were the ones with the sweet tooth. Doughnuts were our reward for getting up early, even though the sun was enough.

Among the first customers at the bakery, we'd fill a box with a dozen soft, warm, sticky treats, mostly chocolate-frosted doughnuts and cinnamon buns, our favorites. We'd try really hard not to eat them on the way home, and we'd grin with anticipation as we pulled up to the house.

On Nunaluk Spit I missed my dad and the easy days of my youth when I could count on my parents to shelter me. When I'd moved to Alaska, I thought it meant asserting my independence. I hadn't considered aging parents or that I might value family differently as I got older. But I'd come to see that the one enormous downside of moving to Alaska was being thousands of miles and an expensive plane ticket from my family. I thought back to the conversation I'd had with Tony and Becky about home and how they were struggling to choose between place and community, and it struck me that I'd failed to incorporate family into my idea of home.

I talked with my parents on the phone every week, and once or twice a year we managed to gather at my brother's house in Southern California. During each visit we made a point to walk down to the beach to watch the sun set over the Pacific Ocean. As Dad approached eighty I couldn't help but wonder how many more sunsets we might have together. There was a thought like a nagging mosquito: if JT and I decided to have a child, I wondered if we'd do it in time for Dad to share a sunset with him or her.

Annoyed to have one more element adding pressure to this decision, I shifted uncomfortably in the sand on Nunaluk Spit. Up until now I'd quietly hoped that JT would change his mind or get distracted with something else, but it was becoming apparent that my strategy of denial wasn't working.

Yesterday evening when I was sitting outside the tent and no one else was around, JT sat down beside me.

"All this down time out here has me thinking more about having kids," he said.

I tensed.

"Have you thought about it some more?" he pressed.

I *had* thought about it and was angry at myself for not being able to find a peaceful resolution. Terrified of losing him and our sweet life, I snapped. "Do you really want kids, or do you just like the *idea* of kids? Do you think kids will make you feel better about your life? I mean, do you know how good you have it? You really want to give all this up? These trips, our time together?"

He looked hurt and turned away.

That day I would have to face him and have something better to say. Sitting on Nunaluk Spit I couldn't imagine an ocean farther from the Jersey Shore. Yet, as the sun hung on the horizon and seagulls swooped and screamed overhead, I felt Dad next to me and had an urge to lick sweet chocolate icing from salty fingers, though there wasn't a doughnut shop for hundreds of miles.

ARCTIC
BEAUTY

A year later I was with Becky again. I could think of no better way
to commemorate ten years of living in Alaska than with a trip
together to one of our favorite places. Before Becky and I launched
toward Matcharak Lake to begin our trip in Gates of the Arctic
National Park, we spent a couple days in Kotzebue, the hub of the
Northwest Arctic. Strolling along the waterfront we passed a house
with a row of six dead caribou strung up in the yard. A neighbor had
rack after rack of drying salmon. Sled dogs tied to six-foot chains lay
tightly curled beside their doghouses. Occasionally someone tossed
a caribou leg within a dog's reach amid dirty hay and dark urine
spots. Houses, just feet from Kotzebue Sound, swam in a sea of car
parts, defunct boats, snowmobile parts, buoys, television sets, tires,
windows, the occasional washing machine, and perhaps a moldering
wooden dogsled.

We ambled to the grocery store to collect a couple of last-minute items, an apple and a bag of tortillas, for our trip. While waiting in line I overheard a woman speak excitedly into her cell phone. "There is so much here!" She must have come from one of the outlying villages, where Kotzebue is the big city, the only place in hundreds of miles with a real grocery and hardware store.

Becky turned to me. "Crazy. To me, this place feels like the edge of the earth."

I felt the same way. After all, the port is ice-free only a couple months a year. There are no roads connecting Kotzebue to any other village. There aren't even summer roads that spike away from it. The nearest town with more than five thousand people is Fairbanks, which is 440 miles away.

We left the grocery store and walked to the Thai restaurant, one of just a handful of places to eat, for one final town meal. We passed both Inupiat and white women dressed in the region's customary attire—colorful parkas with pleated skirts called *kuspuks*. We passed residents speaking Inupiaq, a language that has multiple words to describe conditions of snow, a language rich with place names for thousands of locations throughout millions of acres of their homeland, which some of us now call wilderness.

While Becky and I were waiting for our food we chatted with a small group of locals.

"What kind of work do people do here?" I asked.

One of the young men shrugged. "A lot of people work for government agencies or the Native corporation. I mean, there are artisans too and hunting guides."

Becky asked the young man what he thought about the prospect of a new mine in the region, one of a plethora of resource development projects that were being discussed throughout the Arctic. "If it harms the land, it harms our way of life, our culture," he said. "But my uncle, he says it's good for the economy. He says we need jobs, and these are good jobs."

It didn't sound like there was an overabundance of jobs in the area, which probably explains why, across the Arctic, many people covet the high-paying jobs at Red Dog Mine, the zinc- and lead-mining operation about eighty air miles from Kotzebue and on the oil fields at Prudhoe Bay. Arctic residents, along with the entire United States, look to the coastal plain of the Arctic National Wildlife Refuge to see which side will win the battle: wilderness or oil development. Locals and big conglomerates wait like patient prowling wolves for the next opportunity to make a killing.

———

I pressed my forehead to the window as the little floatplane swooped down onto Matcharak Lake and skidded to a stop against a sliver of shore. We climbed out and let the sunshine hit our faces. It seemed like a good omen, as we were about to spend ten days canoeing a section of the Noatak River, one of the most remote rivers in the world.

We schlepped our gear to the river, assembled the Pakboat (a collapsible canoe), and then dug our heels into the gravel bar and sat back in our camp chairs. The river murmured softly as it slipped over gravel.

"Hey, Bec, what's the latest with the move to McCarthy?"

Becky was upbeat. "We bought the land and are almost done with the yurt, but it's not really going to work to live out there full time without some other structures. Tony's not sure he can pull off being a potter without better access to water. Plus we're still really torn on committing to living out there full time."

"So you might try it for a bit?"

Becky nodded. "We'll probably keep the cabin in Eagle River and spend a couple months in McCarthy this summer and see how it goes."

"Well," I admitted, "selfishly I'm relieved to hear that. How are things going work-wise?" Her job with the Air National Guard was part-time and afforded her considerable flexibility, which made it easier for her to commit to trips, but I knew she'd been searching for something else as well.

"I enjoy the Guard work," she said. "I'm leading a team that's planning for emergency response to natural disasters in Alaska. Did I tell you that I'm going to start working for Revelate Designs sewing bike touring bags?"

"What a fun small team to be part of. Congratulations! What happened to your idea of being a yoga teacher?"

"I'm still looking into it. There's also a Thai massage class I want to take."

"You have a lot of interests."

She smiled. "That's the problem."

JT and I were in the opposite camp. I didn't know what else I would do if I ever had to change careers. Since he'd turned forty, JT had been reevaluating everything, including his teaching job. After a particularly tough day he'd talked about quitting.

"What else would you do?" I'd asked him when we were in a lighter mood.

"Maybe I'd start a business."

"What kind of business?"

He chuckled in defeat. "I don't know."

"So you want to quit your job but have no other ideas?"

He stopped smiling. "I could be a stay-at-home dad."

"Mmm." I gave him a nervous, tightlipped smile.

Just then, an unexpected movement caught my eye. Six caribou appeared out of the willows the way you might imagine ghosts to manifest. The caribou clicked past our camp and hurried into the river holding their antlers high, as if carrying jewels on a platter.

When the pilot had dropped us off, he'd said that the migration was to the east of us and that during the preceding week, the last week in August, as many as two hundred thousand caribou had passed through the tiny village of Anaktuvuk Pass. On the opposite bank, the six caribou shook the river from their fur, like big wet dogs, and carried on clipping across the tundra.

I reclined in my camp chair and considered where Becky and I were in relation to the great expanse of Arctic that covers the northern swath of Alaska. In my mind, the Alaskan Arctic was bookended by the places I've been farthest east (Firth River drainage) and farthest west (Kotzebue). Becky and I sat somewhere in the middle. It was a lot of space to contemplate, a lot of geography to wrap my mind around.

On the Firth River, with JT and a handful of friends, we'd explored nameless mountain ridges on foot and floated on a turquoise ribbon of water between the mountains, into a narrow canyon and across a spidery delta on the coastal plain. During those two weeks on the river, we saw no other people and no signs of humans except for the remnant caribou stick fences that Inuit constructed thousands of years ago to corral caribou to a place where they could be more easily hunted. The Firth River is the easternmost drainage of the Arctic National Wildlife Refuge and consequently the easternmost drainage in northern Alaska. After leaving the headwaters, the river flows into Canada's Yukon Territory and into the Arctic Ocean.

Six hundred miles west of the Firth River is the Noatak River, where Becky and I sat.

"Just imagine, it's the largest river basin in the country," I told her.

"Tony and I have been talking about a trip from Anaktuvuk Pass to Kotzebue, floating the length of either the Noatak or Kobuk." The rivers flow west for about four hundred and three hundred miles, respectively, until they empty into Kotzebue Sound. If Tony and Becky floated out either river delta, across the sound, and hung a left, they'd find themselves in Kotzebue. "We're trying to decide between that and something in the NPR-A."

The National Petroleum Reserve–Alaska is a twenty-three-million-acre tract on the North Slope between Noatak National Preserve and the coast.

"That would be amazing. Did you know Matt just did a trip up there?" I said.

As the grants administrator for the Alaska Conservation Foundation, Matt had taken potential funders to the NPR-A so they could experience firsthand the critical breeding habitat that would be affected by developments and potential contamination associated with oil and gas leasing.

"Yeah," said Becky. "He showed us pictures the other night. He said it felt like the wildest place he'd ever been to. They never even saw a single contrail."

Becky looked across the river and out across endless tundra. "I can't believe we're still drilling in these places," she said. "There has to be a better way to get energy."

Knowing how landscapes like this fill me up, I don't want them to change either.

Becky sighed, then lightened the mood. "Well, in the meantime I guess *someone* has to enjoy these places while they're still pristine."

Strolling to the river's edge Becky searched for stones with interesting patterns, and I looked around for more caribou. We kept coming back to the Arctic to feel the surge of wildness rush through us. And we kept coming back for those rare moments when it was not raining, snowing, blowing hard, or thick with mosquitoes.

After a few days of boating the river, Becky and I found ourselves in one of those rare moments. In the evening, we sat thigh to thigh, facing the river, hands wrapped around mugs of tea. The autumn breeze was cool on my left cheek. I felt my lips chapping from wind and sun—there's nowhere to hide in the wide-open Arctic. We knew that coming into it, which is why we had brought a thermos for tea, hooded down jackets, fleece-lined rubber gloves (for use in the boat), dry suits, and boxy life vests for warmth as much as for flotation.

Our camp looked down on a glassy pool that slid into a riffle. In the evening light I watched flies tag the water's skin. Over the cobbles, where the water rippled, slanted light caught each dimple, making the water shine like sequins. In that moment it felt to me that the rich purple hues along the river and those billions of red and yellow leaves blanketing the Arctic in every direction were solely a testament to God's inclination toward beauty.

"Hey, A," Becky said softly. "I'm sorry I haven't asked you about this in a while, but it's been on my mind. Have you and JT made a decision about kids?"

I paused, and suddenly my chest felt tight as I recalled my last conversation with my husband.

JT had sat beside me on the couch and said he'd been thinking a lot about having a family. "I don't think my life will feel complete without kids," he'd told me. His voice had wavered. "So I guess I need to know where you stand because I'm sure about it."

For a moment I'd stopped breathing, unable to fully process his words. "So," I'd said finally. "What happens if I don't want to have kids?"

JT's face had flushed. "I don't think it's an option for me," he'd said.

I'd started to cry, but he didn't hug me. "Can you give me some more time?" I'd said.

He had said he could.

I turned to Becky. "He might leave me if I don't want to have kids."

Becky's eyes widened. She didn't say anything.

Tears came to my eyes. "Life has been so good," I lamented, remembering when it felt like JT loved me more than anything in the world. "I don't want it to change."

For a few minutes neither of us tried to find words to backfill the space my sadness had created. It was a relief to simply watch the water.

When our tea was gone we cooked dinner over our camp stove and joked about actually having a stove this year. In fact, because we could carry more in a boat than in a backpack, we carried two stoves, just in case.

We lounged with heaping bowls of lentil soup and looked in every direction.

"Did you see the bear and wolf tracks where they crossed the beach beside the river?" asked Becky.

"Yeah, I did." I wondered how those big animals stayed out of sight in such open country. If we wanted to see more wildlife, we'd have to be good stalkers or very lucky because everything was ducking and hiding or running away.

We froze at the exact same moment, having heard an unmistakable sound. First one wolf howled, and then there were others. I grinned at Becky, and we closed our eyes. The sound was deep and rich and haunting. How bold, in such a quiet place, where other creatures seemed to work so hard at being discreet, to fill all that space with sound. A feeling ignited inside me, a feeling that had nothing to do with the tangible "resources" I wrote about at work.

The wolves paused, and I turned to Becky. "I love this."

"How many do you think there are?" she whispered.

I shrugged.

"How far away?" she wondered.

"Not that far," I said, buzzing from the experience. "We're so lucky."

We continued eating dinner. As I looked across the Arctic plains it was easy to feel like we were the first people to experience the landscape, easy to cling to the idea of untouched wilderness void of human impact. But where the hand of modern humans *has* touched the Arctic, it's left a big print. The Dalton Highway and the Trans-Alaska

Pipeline cut a vertical line through the middle of the Arctic. When I looked at aerial images of Red Dog Mine and traveled to Deadhorse, the gateway to Prudhoe Bay, I was astounded that humans could create such apocalyptic scenes in the middle of the most pristine wilderness on earth. The dusty air, engines revving and grinding, huge trucks, fences, elevated development pads, and roads built over the wet tundra are a drastic contrast to the surrounding areas. At the airport in Deadhorse, when I'd asked the airline agent if there was an earlier flight out, she'd just chuckled and said, "People will pay almost anything to get out of here earlier."

I can't imagine more of the Arctic meeting that same fate. But there are more proposed mines, proposed roads to serve them, and a hunger to drill in the coastal plain of the Arctic Refuge, not to mention the NPR-A enticing speculative companies.

My friends who work for British Petroleum and Conoco Phillips in Anchorage say, "Better here where we have environmental laws in place than in China or Russia, where almost anything goes."

More compelling to me than the "it could be worse" argument is the simple fact that I personally required so much energy to live in Alaska. The logical part of my brain said, "We need energy to sustain our way of life, and energy has to come from somewhere. Think of all the energy it takes to ship my bananas from Chile, the building supplies for my house, my car and the fuel it takes to drive it, every single item I use." Virtually nothing is manufactured in Alaska. It all comes from somewhere else, and of course it takes resources not only to make the things that support my lifestyle but also to transport them to me over long distances. What a hypocrite I was—hoping that the oil companies would keep their hands off my wilderness while I munched up countless times more energy than practically everyone else in the world. Not every wild place could remain unchanged, I guessed, for me to continue my lifestyle. But I could change too. Most of the drilling and all of the coal mining wouldn't be necessary if we invested in renewable energy, fuel-efficient vehicles, and public transportation and if we committed, as best we could, to eating locally. There was room in my own life to make some adjustments.

I found it interesting that Alaskan culture had shifted a number of strongly held opinions I'd come here with, but it hadn't been able to ease the heartache I felt at the thought of bulldozing a road through wilderness to reach a mining operation. The Luddite in me felt like technology and development kept threatening my beloved landscapes in new and faster ways, and my fear of this had only heightened since moving to Alaska. The stakes were higher here. There was more to lose, and we only have to lose once and we've lost wildness forever. The part of me that acknowledges that energy must come from somewhere won't flex to the part of me that believes these places will be worth so much more if we leave them just the way they are for another thousand years.

—————

A few days later along the river, all Becky and I saw were caribou antlers. Each rogue willow branch, stick, and rock on a ridgeline looked like antlers. In the course of one long afternoon that stretched into evening, we watched hundreds of caribou file past our camp. In one group, all I saw were pink antlers, bloody from the annual shedding of velvet. A dozen enormous antlers in a big hurry moved in unison along the top of a bluff. They were grouped so tightly I almost expected to hear their racks clacking like armor. It reminded me of an old war movie in which a soldier looks across the prairie and suddenly thousands of men appear where an instant before there'd been only waving grass. Now the grass is crawling and alive with footfalls, armor clanking, and battle cries.

The caribou came into view when they crested the top of the bluff above the river, and then they cascaded down the steep slope to the edge of the water. Without hesitation they plunged into the river and ran through the current. We heard splashing from our tent as they churned the water white. We heard their hooves tapping river cobbles as they hurried toward the far bank. Pausing to shake the water from their fur, they caught the scent trail from preceding groups and bolted up into the tundra.

I eyeballed the kill zone on a passing caribou. When I remembered how sharing caribou meat made me feel closer to my community, and how cooking with it deepened my thankfulness for food, killing these creatures seemed easy to justify.

I had been on two other hunts since my first one, and while we had ended up taking an animal each time, I hadn't been the one to pull the trigger, which had been a relief. On one of the hunts, Tony and I had stalked a caribou for more than an hour, up and down a valley, tracking it as it emerged from thick brush and trying to anticipate where it was headed. Sometimes we'd thought we were seeing two different animals, and the brush made it hard to tell. When finally it had crested a ridge, I'd sat still and waited to see if there was a second one. As I debated whether or not to go ahead and shoot it, the other had come into view. It was a calf, and it had walked to its mother and nuzzled her neck. They'd stood nose to nose, and the cow had guided the calf down to the ground where they curled up together. Less than fifty feet away from them, Tony and I lay side by side grinning to have witnessed such a beautiful moment. I put the rifle down.

"We're not going to kill a caribou today," I'd whispered.

"No," he'd agreed. "Not today."

This is how I would forever think of caribou, how Becky and I saw them that day: white necks and rich brown bodies, white antlers rubbed down to bone that shines in the slanted Arctic light. No time to rest. With ground to cover, their quick legs part yellow alders and blood-red blueberry bushes. Their strong, lithe bodies are made perfectly for this landscape. Tussocks that Becky and I stumbled over for an hour, the caribou crossed in a matter of minutes.

Group after group came from the north and crossed the Noatak River. Emerging in front of or behind our tent, they paid us about as much attention as they did a willow. There were hundreds, some brazen, some cautious. Spindly calves swam behind their mothers and mimicked their moms' kicks and shakes and snorts. That night I dreamed that thousands of caribou were stampeding across what looked like the Serengeti, all dust and hooves and sweaty grunts, which wasn't anything like what Becky and I had witnessed. In the dream, Becky and I lined up with cameras, and the caribou parted around us like water around a rock. Who knows how many caribou passed our tent during the night. Perhaps that's what really happened.

The following morning we nudged the canoe into the current, and a group of caribou entered the water and swam across the river less than one hundred yards in front of our boat. Around the bend we spotted a big glossy grizzly bear walking on the edge of the rise about ten feet above the river. I thought I might have been able to stick my hand into his chocolate-brown coat and not touch skin. His hide rippled as he walked. We quickly ferried to the opposite bank to give him space. In no hurry, the bear sat down and looked around. When we proceeded downriver, hugging the opposite bank, the bear slowly swung his big head in our direction and watched us float past.

The river swept us out into open country where there was water before us and sky all around. We startled a dark brown fox clipping along the bank. He paused to watch us in much the same way as the bear and then leaped up above the bank on paws soft as cotton. Without making a sound, he hovered as much as ran across the tundra, his movements precise as a cat's, his gait crisp and quick. At a safe distance he pointed his nose our way, sat down, and wrapped his bushy tail across his body like a scarf to astutely observe our passing.

A while later we paddled into a crosswind toward what looked like a pile of boulders, when one of the boulders moved.

"Is that a bear?" I asked Becky.

"It's big and brown," she said squinting, "but it doesn't seem like a bear."

The blob turned sort of blocky, and it wasn't until the bow of our boat nearly hit the gravel shore twenty yards away that the brown block stood up.

"Whoa," I said nervously as the image suddenly computed: three hulky musk oxen. The one on the left squared its prehistoric head toward us and grunted. The other two pulled themselves off the ground to standing, curvy horns framing their faces like George Washington's hairdo.

"How close should we be?" Becky whispered.

I was surprised to realize that I had no idea. Would they charge us like a bear might? Would they run away? Embarrassed that I didn't know much about musk oxen, I suggested that we quietly ferry back into the current.

We didn't take our eyes off them, though. Their profiles resembled the outline of a slice of bread, and their coats looked like shag carpet circa 1973. We watched each other for a few long moments until they turned on their heels and humped toward the willows, close together. Then they turned to assess us once more before disappearing into the brush.

A few days later, on the final evening of our trip, sunlight angled low on the horizon. The clouds turned pink. The riverbanks glowed yellow and red, and for a moment I felt warmth from the sun on my face. Then it was gone. We stood in shadow, and I spun around. Our cold camp was ringed by softly lit horizons. Soon it would be dark. Always changing, this landscape, hour to hour. Compelling us to adapt. A chill seeped through to my clammy skin. I pulled my hood over my hat and turned my attention to my water bottle filled with hot water. Putting it at the foot of my sleeping bag was the greatest luxury in the world.

I woke a couple hours later needing to pee. Too much tea after dinner. Orange light glowed on the western horizon. I walked to the edge of the river, and two snowy owls swooped over my head. How do they fly without making a sound? I saw their heads turn, their eyes watching me. I turned toward the river to linger a moment more, and in a swatch of sunset that was bright and colorless like moonlight I saw two egrets skimming the water, their flight reflected on the calm surface. The pair passed directly in front of me, and I realized that it is the birds that enchant the Arctic, the way they fill the wide-open space, the only creatures that can.

I wanted this moment to last forever. I wanted to suspend time. I wanted places like our camp by the river to endure, with scenes of snowy owls, chocolate grizzly bears, and howling wolves playing out for generations to come. It's easy to want it to stay this way. Just as it's easy to want to suspend chapters in time when we were at our best, when love spread like soft butter, when decisions flowed like unfettered Arctic rivers. It's easy sometimes to want more than I know I'll get.

IT HAPPENED LIKE THIS

JT and I had spent little time together that summer. He and Tony had been on climbing trips while I'd had to work. Other times my job had taken me out to the parks and I'd left JT behind. The distance between us had forestalled any decision about children, although we both knew that we couldn't keep avoiding it. I'd missed his company and was delighted when JT suggested we spend the day together on the Portage River. I was grateful for his continued attempts to reconcile, to draw me out. He was not giving up on us.

The water sparkled, and a light breeze settled the bugs. It was so serene my heart ached. I lay down across the front of the raft with my head hovering over the water and watched big pink wiggling salmon swim upstream under the boat: slippery bodies and thrashing tails, suspended midstream. I thought I could almost walk across their backs, and I tried to imagine balancing barefoot on a slippery muscular flotilla of fish.

"Wouldn't it be great to be able to share something like this with kids?" said JT with a slight smile.

He seemed lost in a fantasy, which I guessed was about taking children rafting and witnessing the expression on their faces as they encountered fish as big as these.

"I don't know," I said quietly, looking down.

JT straightened and changed his tone. "When do you think you'll know?"

It felt like the hundredth time we'd had this conversation.

"Having kids is a really big deal," I said. "Things would never be the same."

"Yeah, and—?"

We'd been talking for almost two years about having children, and I was determined to be honest with myself. If I really didn't want children, bringing a child into the world would be a terrible thing to do. But what if we were missing out?

I reflected on the way several of my friends had looked at me. It had taken me a while to realize it was a look of pity. I noticed it was often accompanied with some iteration of this: "I can't explain how amazing it is. You just have no idea until you do it."

Coming from people I trusted, it had made me wonder, and so for the first time in my life, the thought of my freedom and independence being eroded was, if only in fleeting moments, countered by the possibility of something intriguing. But I'd had to ask myself, "Would it be fun to become a bigger family, or am I trying to talk myself into it because I don't want JT to leave me?"

On the Portage River with JT, I stared into the water, wishing for an answer.

A few months earlier Corrina had asked if I'd come to the birthing center for the birth of her daughter.

"Are you sure I'm the best choice?" I'd responded. "You know I'm not even sure I like kids, right?"

"We could use a calm presence," she'd said.

I'd consented, and then I helped her. I rubbed her back as she moaned in unfathomable pain. I helped her change positions. I held her quivering body as her little girl passed out of her and into the world.

JT afterward had asked if being part of the birth had changed my feelings about having kids.

"It was both miraculous and arresting," I'd told him, "and unfortunately I don't think it affected my personal decision at all." However I looked at it, I arrived at the same conclusion: birth is a small, albeit significant, moment in time. My concerns about having kids had more to do with what happens during the rest of my life than with what happens during that one excruciating, terrifying, exhausting, transcendent, unbelievable, beautiful day.

JT and I returned from the river and had dinner without saying much. I was reminded of an evening not too long before, when my parents were visiting. We'd sat around the living room looking at each other. It wasn't necessarily that we had run out of things to talk about. I just had the sense that something was missing. Everyone had politely agreed they were tired and went to bed early.

That night after the day on the Portage River I went to bed early but couldn't sleep. Like a rapid in front of an approaching raft, the time for decision was upon us. Do we go left, or do we go right? Irritably, I admitted to myself that I was not a *passenger* on this raft— I was the one holding the oars. I couldn't sit back and watch life float by. No one else could make this decision. I had to make it myself. But I needed a sign, an epiphany, some help.

In the morning, after JT left on a trip, I tried to meditate. I'd been practicing when home alone. I felt self-conscious about it, coming as I do from an agnostic upbringing and a history of faith in the scientific method. But the wilderness all around me had made me feel forces greater than those explainable by science. In the wild, something inside me opens to innovation, inspiration, creativity, and imagination. It's a good feeling, one that leaves me light and full of energy, free to imagine who I want to be in this life, but it's slippery and ephemeral, and I can never seem to pack it out with me.

So I sat on the bed, stared up at the green slopes of Threebowls, and tried to focus on being open. It was mostly frustrating. It felt like I'd been sitting for thirty minutes, but the clock told me it had been only five.

The following day I decided to practice outside. I put my backpack on, walked out the door, and headed up the valley with August at my side. I stepped around bright pink fireweed and watched the creek flow past me in the opposite direction. It was warm and it didn't take me long to heat up, loosen, and find a pleasant pace. I focused on the weight of each footfall and the rhythm of my breath. I planned to walk a few hours to an unnamed tarn above Symphony Lake and camp. I had plenty of time to think.

Hours passed, and I approached the headwaters. Something nagged at me, something I kept replaying in my mind. It had happened a couple months earlier, and I hadn't shared it with anyone. Determined to continue taking significant chunks of time away from the office to, as Page had advised, "practice for retirement," I had traveled by myself to Peru. In Cusco I had toured the city and surrounding archaeological sites and met a big boisterous family. They had invited me into their lives, and I'd stopped traveling and moved in with them for a couple of weeks. I ate with them and cooked with them and celebrated a birthday and was there when Carmen, the Quechua grandmother, got angry and chased her grown son through the house with a wooden club. I played soccer in the street with the kids and visited their school.

One day all of the adults had gone to work, and they'd left me in charge of three young kids who didn't speak English. Little Carmencita asked me to hold her hand and go first into the dark bedroom to get her T-shirt. She looked up at me with big brown eyes and confided, "I'm scared of the dark." Seven-year-old Lalito insisted we play Monopoly, and he misinterpreted my not understanding the language as not understanding the game. Patiently he helped me move my piece around the board and pay for land. Ryan, the littlest, crawled into my lap and rested his head on my thigh.

Another morning the grandmother had told me she was taking me into town. She'd held my hand in the taxi and asked if I had children. When I said no, she shook her head and demanded I tell her the truth.

"No," I insisted. "I don't have children." I hadn't known what else to say. After spending endearing moments with her grandchildren, it didn't feel right to tell her that I didn't really like kids.

It had taken the entire taxi ride to convince her that I was being truthful.

Looking disoriented, she'd finally conceded. "You're just such a natural mother, I thought—"

———

At the headwaters, I crested the last green rise and was level with the turquoise lake and the slim twist of water flowing out of it. Here the creek is so narrow that I jumped over it. I turned my gaze toward the cirque in front of me, rimmed by cliffs on three sides. Dall sheep traversed vertical chutes above the lake. Sunlight splashed all around. August curled into a ball and closed his eyes.

I set my backpack beside me, drank some water, and sat down. At once I felt so comfortable in this place, in my skin. I began to breathe slowly, consciously. Surprisingly, my attention easily turned to my breath and the stillness in the rest of my body. I noticed a breeze ever so gently tickle the hair on my arm and touch my cheek. Then

I was outside my body, looking at myself sitting beside the lake. All that was left was awareness. That awareness was like a band wrapping around the valley, over the mountains, across Alaska, and stretching all the way around the globe. I inhaled awareness of all the energy of all living things around the planet, and when it felt like it was too much to take in, I kept going. I expanded my awareness to the solar system, and then I let that feeling extend to as many galaxies as I could imagine, far out into the blackness of space.

There was no time where I was. There was only a strange and delicious sense of knowing that I had reached out to the universe and that it touched me back.

I inhaled. I exhaled. Energy coursed around me.

Then, lightly, I came back down until I was a girl sitting on the tundra. Yet I was indistinguishable from the tundra. The wind flowed through me. The earth's breath was the gentle breeze that became mine. We were sustaining each other.

From this brief meditation I did not gain an epiphany, but I lay back on the earth feeling satisfied.

I sat quietly beside the lake, absorbing the last echoes of that pulsing energy, and I thought about a friend of mine who'd told me that, to her, going into what we call wilderness is an opportunity to feel the footsteps of her Dena'ina ancestors. I tend to think about wilderness as devoid of humans, and I gain something important from that reference point, but I also sense that there is a depth to her connection that maybe I don't have. I envy her attachment to her homeland. She seems not only connected to the mountains but to the people who have inhabited the land for thousands of years, people with whom she shares a past, people with whom she shares blood and stories and spirits. What must that be like to feel that you can reach back in time and ask all the mothers in your bloodline how they made the decision to have children?

Much later that night, around midnight, when it was still bright as midday and the shirt I'd put over my eyes to block the sunshine had fallen off, I got up and went for a walk. I looked back down the valley for miles and wondered how many animals there were that I couldn't see. I couldn't tell which clump of willows hid the bear, the moose, and the wolf, but their tracks crisscrossed swatches of mud and snow patches. I felt like I should see a coyote loping across the valley or stalking a nest on the ground, maybe crouching to drink from one of the tiny kettle puddles in the folds sloping below the lake.

I felt so small walking through all that space in the middle of the night, and once again I sensed that it might be easy to feel connected to something larger, something eternal—to the people who had passed through this same land thousands of years ago. Where did my own ancestors wander, and what did they do? I'd never done this before, but I called upon them for guidance, for some insight into the decision that lay in my path. If nothing else, for reassurance that when I'm at the lip of the rapid I'll have the capacity to steer right or left.

In that moment, asking for help seemed like the right thing to do. It seemed that out there in all of that quiet space my grandmothers might hear me. More importantly, free from societal norms and constraints, free from duties and obligations, free from the burden of technology, and free from the reminders of all the things I manage in my life, maybe finally I would hear *them*.

CONSEQUENCES

When I moved to Alaska, people warned me about the cold and the darkness. What they didn't warn me about was how hard it might be for a liberal-leaning individual to grow roots in a largely conservative state. At first I noticed the bumper stickers, the ones that claimed PETA stood for "People Eating Tasty Animals" and others that declared "Earth First! We'll strip mine the other planets later." Later I began to notice how the state's population rallied around oil and gas development with a religious fervor. I witnessed the mortifying release of Sarah Palin into the world, efforts to open new coal mines while polar bears drowned trying to swim between melting patches of sea ice, weekly reports of people shooting any bear they saw and claiming they were defending themselves, and the state government's solicitation of pilot-gunner teams to fly over the Alaska tundra and shoot wolves from airplanes. I would come to be astounded by Alaskans who say they don't believe in climate change, even though I have seen things change right out my backdoor. Over the years, JT and I have watched the brush get thicker behind our house, shallow ponds dry, and glaciers retreat. There is no question that things are changing quickly, more quickly here than in most parts of the world.

Not only was my external environment changing, so too was my internal one. I came to Alaska in my twenties, unhindered by relationships or a permanent job. I chased dreams of saving wild places while embarking upon endless exploration of remote mountain wilderness. After a dozen years I found myself with a career, not just a summer job. I found myself with a husband and a house and the reality that wild places take a lot more effort to preserve than I had imagined. So did my evolving sense of who I am.

———

JT and I were strolling through the neighborhood after dinner. He had a sad look in his eyes, like he might start to cry. "I can't wait any longer," he told me.

I'd been anticipating this. I hooked my arm through his.

"You're going to think I'm crazy," I replied softly.

"Yeah, what else is new?"

"Maybe we could sort of stop birth control and see how it goes."

For a few seconds his mouth was open in disbelief, and then he retrieved his humor. "Are you sure you didn't just bang your head real hard? Fall off your bike or something?"

Somewhat sheepishly I told JT that I thought I'd confronted a lot of my fears. "I don't think backing off our wilderness adventures is the end of the world anymore."

As I'd meditated more, I had been posing a question to myself, "What if I said yes to a baby?" Over time, I had observed that saying "yes" had begun to make my body feel more curious than afraid. I wondered if part of my reluctance had been fear of losing the naïve, steadfast version of myself that I had become attached to. And I wondered whether my anger toward JT wasn't actually a reflection of my anger at myself. "Children compromise a woman's ability to wring the nectar from life," I'd asserted. And I'd clung to that. But I had finally come to admit that maybe that tenet no longer served me. Maybe *not* having a baby was constraining the breadth of my life experiences.

What ultimately swayed me was that I didn't want to miss out on what my Alaska friends with kids told me I couldn't even fathom. I didn't want to miss the joy of children that I'd witnessed in the Peruvian family's household, the beauty of seeing my parents as grandparents and my brother as an uncle. Alaska probably had something to do with it too—this place that has kept inspiring me to push against my edges and experience as much of the human condition as I can.

JT hugged me with tears in his eyes. I was surprised he didn't ask more about my transformation. Maybe he was afraid to revisit it now that he'd finally gotten the answer he wanted.

"Have you thought about names?" he asked excitedly.

"Names?" I said. I hadn't thought about anything beyond the decision to try to have a baby.

JT quickened the pace. "If we have a girl I have a bunch of ideas. Boys' names, those are harder. Oh! But I do have one idea. I don't know if you'll like it, though."

He gestured with both hands open like stars. "Which room should be the kid's room? I was first thinking the office, but now I think the guest room would be better because of the closet."

Not a week later Holly called, and she was talking so fast I could hardly understand her.

"I have news," she blurted out. "You're not going to believe it."

The receiver was pressed to my ear, and I felt her smiling her gigantic smile, and I heard that nervous and excited lilt in her voice, and I knew immediately, the way only soul sisters know.

"You're pregnant." I said.

"How did you know?" she said.

Of course I'd know, it occurred to us both.

And without even thinking I said, "You know how usually I tell people I'm excited for them when they're pregnant, but actually I'm not?"

"Yeah," she chuckled.

"Holly." I could barely get the words out as tears trickled down my cheek. "I'm really, really happy for you."

———

A couple months later JT and I counted the days until we would check to see if I was pregnant. I held the stick like a prize and jumped up and down when it indicated I was. JT kissed me, and we made a halibut dinner together to celebrate. We found a website that told us what to expect every week of the pregnancy, and we sat side by side and read every word.

A few weeks later we went to a show in town. Being out in public felt different now, like I was up to something special. We hadn't told anyone, and I was far from showing, but I sat there laughing at the performance and giddy that I had a wonderful secret.

During intermission I used the restroom and happened to glance at the tissue before I threw it in the toilet. A blotch of blood on the tissue made me break into a panicky sweat. I pushed open the restroom door and emerged into a crowd of friends. I ignored their greetings and nervously scanned the crowd for JT.

"We need to go now," I told him.

"What is—" he whispered to my back as he trailed me to the door.

Outside, my eyes welled up. "The baby," I said, burying my eyes in his chest. "There was blood."

———

We tried again. And again. We shared our struggle with some of our closest friends and found it to be a complicated balance. Losing a baby and not being able to get pregnant are isolating experiences, but making our losses public seemed like it would create more of a burden. So we only told our families and a few friends. Becky, Tony, and Matt came over to comfort us and bring dinner.

"I'm really honored you shared that with us," said Tony, "I mean, if we ever try to have kids I'm not sure if we'd tell anyone or not. It seems hard either way."

"Wait," I said, loving that they'd given us an opportunity to redirect the conversation. "You're going to have kids? Are you getting married too?"

Tony flushed, and Becky laughed and looked at him.

"Commitment," Matt jeered. "So scary."

The next day Corrina took me on a walk. "I guess what losing the baby has showed me," I told her, "is that I actually do want to have a baby."

"Now that you finally want this and can't have it, does it feel kind of insulting?" she asked.

"Yeah, like *what is the universe doing?*"

JT and I found a fertility specialist named Joy. Even when she wore high heels she barely came up to my chest, but her mighty presence filled the room.

"We're going to figure this out," she declared as a matter of fact, and I believed her.

She ran tests and ordered blood draws. In her office she flipped through my chart, tracking her notes with long fingernails painted in pretty designs. She adjusted her gold necklaces and without looking up said, "I'm putting you on—" and named a drug I'd never heard of. "You have a thyroid condition, and there could be something else going on too." She explained the interplay of hormones and my physiology, using words I couldn't spell. "This treatment hasn't been officially accepted," she said, "But I've studied enough clinical trials to see a pattern." I didn't know what questions I should be asking, so I elected to nod and trust her.

She stood up to walk me to the door and pulled me in for a great big hug. "We're going to figure this out, okay?"

The drugs I started taking were supposed to help me get pregnant and prevent my body from rejecting the fetus. I changed my diet. I stopped all activities that demanded anything more than a low level of physical exertion. No backpacking. No backcountry skiing. I was exhausted one minute, overly anxious about work the next. I yelled at JT when he left a light on, then felt weepy the rest of the night. I reassured myself these were only temporary sacrifices for a greater long-term goal.

———

One Saturday morning Joy called, and I could see her smiling through the phone. "You're pregnant!" she exclaimed.

"I can't believe it!" I told her, nearly jumping up and down.

"Now take it easy," she said. "You'll come in every week for tests. Don't start telling everyone you know. And no running up any mountains, okay?"

"What do you think about my work trip to Kotzebue next week? It's a river patrol that—"

"On the blood thinners? What kind of advanced medical facilities do they have up there?"

I recalled my friend Dave, who lives in Kotzebue, telling me how he used to sneak his dogs into the hospital for X-rays. "Not very good ones I guess?" I replied timidly.

"You were really thinking of going to Kotzebue?"

"Well," I confessed, "not Kotzebue exactly but the backcountry about a hundred miles from—"

"Absolutely not," she said, and that was the end of that.

A couple weeks later Dad came to visit, so we shared the great news with him. At the end of his visit, on the way to the airport, we stopped at a café for dessert. Joy called as we were waiting in line for thick slices of chocolate cake.

"Your hCG went down," she said in a tender voice. "Come in tomorrow and we'll run labs again, but it doesn't look good."

I joined JT and Dad at the table, suddenly revolted by food, staring at hunks of chocolate cake.

Between trembling lips I managed to repeat Joy's words, "It doesn't look good."

We asked for to-go containers and drove to the airport in silence. We left Dad at the curb clutching his suitcase, with tears in his eyes.

It seemed too ironic that I, who had resisted having a child for so long, now wanted this more than anything but might not be able to have one. A childless future seemed as impossible to imagine as whole glaciers melting in my lifetime.

I got up the next morning and snapped at JT, "Close the bathroom door! What's wrong with you?" I wanted him to feel angry too, but instead he brushed it off.

"We're going to get through this," he said sweetly.

I burst out crying for no apparent reason other than not liking who I'd become. JT hugged me, and I laughed until my body shuddered.

I wondered if everything we were doing was worth it. My body felt contaminated with drugs, my emotions taken over by the highs and lows of pregnancy and hormone supplements. I needed to get off the drugs. I needed my life to stop revolving around blood draws and popping pills. Maybe I needed to come to terms with the lot we'd been dealt. I was thirty-eight years old. Maybe I needed to accept that I wouldn't be able to have a biological child after all. The questions loomed: When is enough, enough? If not now, when?

The tipping point in my own life was mirrored by a global dilemma, which we talked about a lot at work. Those changes that had been happening in my backyard—the melting glaciers, the thicker brush, the drying ponds—people were beginning to ask if we should do anything about it. Not just reduce our carbon emissions to correct the root of the problem but also actually physically do anything constructive about it. In a meeting at the NPS office in Anchorage, my colleague Peter pondered these changes. "In a warming climate how long will polar bears be able to survive in the Arctic?"

John chimed in, "The Dall sheep alpine habitat is being invaded by trees. How much longer will they be able to persist?"

On the Kenai Peninsula, the site of my first caribou hunt, land managers were talking about aggressively using herbicides to kill invasive plants, perhaps moving deer to the peninsula because caribou may not fare so well in the future, and releasing genetically modified disease-resistant salmon. I thought about how magical that hunt had felt because it had occurred where Mother Earth made the rules more than humans had. I had participated in a landscape and ecosystem that had been evolving unimpeded for eons. If the animal I'd been hunting had been brought in from elsewhere and the mountain slope I had belly-crawled over had been mowed, I doubt if I would have felt as strong a connection to nature as I did.

Peter, an ecologist, twirled a pen between his fingers. "It's tricky because humans have already manipulated most of the planet. Alaska wilderness is one of the only places we haven't intentionally tried to alter. There's value to science to be able to study what happens if nature is allowed to evolve on its own. It's also what wilderness areas are about, letting things be, right?" He looked at me. Over the preceding year I'd begun to specialize in wilderness issues for the national parks in Alaska. I nodded at Peter.

John straightened up. "But we have to fight back against climate change."

I thought about it. The plants and animals that have historically occupied our parks might not be able to live there in the future. But to save a certain species, what would it take? And what would the process of saving one animal species do to the rest of the ecosystem? In the Alaska national parks, what type of treatment would be acceptable to apply?

I considered the Dall sheep and turned to John. "What would you do about it, though? Cut the trees down so the sheep have desirable habitat? Move them to a higher range of mountains? Fence out their predators so they have a better chance?"

"Whatever it takes," he said. "It could mean relocating sheep, fencing out predators, altering their habitat. I know some people are talking about bigger things, like putting blankets on glaciers to slow the melting, fertilizing the oceans, injecting sulfur dioxide into the stratosphere to reflect the sun's rays back into space, spraying seawater into clouds above the ocean to increase their reflectivity and consequently their cooling effect. I wouldn't rule them out."

In my mind I could hear my mom singing to me when I was a little girl: "She swallowed the dog to catch the cat, she swallowed the cat to catch the bird, she swallowed the bird to catch the spider that wiggled and jiggled and tickled inside her, she swallowed the spider to catch the fly, I don't know why she swallowed the fly."

"If we don't," John continued, his eyes wide with fear, "we're going to see massive loss of plants and animals and species suddenly living together that shouldn't."

I imagine that it's for the same reason—our collective fear of death and large changes—that we tend to keep elderly people alive even after major organs have all but called it quits. Technology will postpone death, they say, as if dying of old age has become an offense. Technology may postpone death but often not without preventing a person from dying naturally with dignity. Easy to say, I suppose, and harder to decide. On what day do you draw the line? Which medical procedure is one too many?

My body seemed to be telling me that it was not possible to have a baby. My doctors said it was, to just let them try something. But at what point has *something* gone too far? After how many cycles of drugs would I start losing something vital to me being myself? I was recognizing that Western medicine with its bias toward action would always offer hope. It would be up to me to take the oars and determine when I felt too much like a science experiment and too little like myself to continue.

But the wilderness doesn't have the same power I do, to call a halt before we kill its spirit. I wonder what we sacrifice as a society if we intentionally manipulate every inch of the planet. What part of our collective spiritual composition is lost when we spray poison onto the places that we've deemed most sacred, like our national parks, in order to save a certain species of flower? What falls away from our identity as Americans when the last wild vestiges of the frontier are fenced and fertilized?

At home that evening, JT and I shared a grilled salmon dinner and I told him about my day at work. "Saving Mother Nature sounds pretty good at first," I told him. "But it seems to come dangerously close to playing God."

He looked at me, contemplating this. "Or at least Noah," he said. "How many species can we fit in our ark?"

"No offense to humanity, but I don't think we're capable of orchestrating a successful reconfiguration of nature on a global scale, whether that's carting around deer or blanketing glaciers."

"Hmmm," he wondered. "How would you do that here?" How *would* you halt the effects of a changing climate in a twelve-million-acre park?

"I don't think it's possible," I contended. "I don't think climate change is something we will be able to heal. Over the long haul we'll ultimately be overwhelmed by the synergistic effect of numerous global changes, everything from temperature to precipitation, patterns of ocean currents, and length of the growing season. I wish that in Alaska, where nature is so intact, that we would let Mother Earth own her own response to a changing climate."

I felt frustrated that more people didn't seem to understand, as JT and I did, that there's value in a land ethic that emphasizes respect for nature as a self-willed entity. Could we try, in some places, to adapt our inner emotional landscapes and expectations instead of forcing nature to bend, once again, to our will?

The adventures I'd had in Alaska, from hunting caribou on the Kenai Peninsula to traversing glaciers in the Lake Clark region and floating Arctic rivers, were meaningful to me not because of which species of plants and animals have historically been there but because I touched the spirit of a place that had been allowed to evolve on its own, without humans crashing through the gate with our garden tools. Places like the Arctic National Wildlife Refuge have a powerful energy. They evoke something deep and transformative in me, and that power is lost when the spirit of the land is broken by our meddling, even if we call it healing. I value the functioning ecosystems, biodiversity, and ecosystem services of the Arctic Refuge, but I appreciate inspiration, humility, restraint, and mystery even more. I appreciate how we honor the land, how we defer to it, because that keeps it whole. I need to know there's something whole out there, so that I might feel whole too.

I'd realized on my climbs with JT, hiking and boating with Shelley, and Arctic treks and canoe trips with Becky, that it is these social values, not the ecological ones, that lift my spirit. I need the feeling of awe that wells up inside me when I meet the natural world on its own terms, the reverence that reverberates in my bones in a place we've chosen not to change.

Is spirit, or essence, too big a thing to lose in order to save one of the components of an ecosystem? I was still trying to figure out the answer for my own body. I had the power to make choices about manipulating my own ecosystem. Should I continue fighting infertility with drugs, or could I accept my body as it was? I wondered how much of myself I could compromise, how many losses I could endure, while maintaining faith in the future.

MYSTERY

Way up in the northwest corner of the Arctic, a tiny plane lifted off, leaving JT and me in a cloud of mosquitoes. We tore open our backpacks, dug out our head nets, and began searching for a flat patch of ground to pitch the tent, our refuge from the bugs. A raft of mosquitoes perched on the outside of my head net. All I heard was their high-pitched whine. JT's cream-colored shirt was polka-dotted with black insects. There might have been a hundred on his back. There were at least ten biting my hand. I put gloves on, even though the sun was beating down. Distracted by a patch of warm, ripe blueberries, JT knelt to sample a few. I wished to lounge on the pretty green bench of tundra all afternoon stuffing blueberries into our mouths, but as we raked our fingers through the bushes we quickly realized our handfuls were equal parts berries and bugs.

Despite the mosquitoes, there was something special about being in a place we knew little about. We knew that locals—northwestern Alaskans—called the patch of tundra where we'd landed the Copter Peak strip. We also knew that there were no trails, signs, or bridges, and very few officially named peaks and valleys. That was part of the lure of this trip. It was the unknown that made me shimmy my ski tips a little closer to the edge, nudge my shoes forward, and nose the kayak into the current. With all the internet blogs and forums, YouTube videos, and Google Earth maps, it had gotten harder to get this feeling of being in a blank spot on the map.

JT and I quickly pitched our tent and started sorting gear—things we'd carry with us on a day hike and items that would stay in the tent. We unzipped the tent door for each other and swatted at mosquitoes while the other got organized. It felt good to be a team again in the backcountry.

Taking advantage of the lightness between us, I called to JT. "Hey, did you know that my high school mascot was the Pioneer? We were the Conestoga Pioneers."

"We were the Larrys, if that makes you feel any better."

"What's a Larry?"

"Just a guy named Larry," he laughed. "Yeah, I know."

"Right. Well, it just reminded me of this school project where we pretended we were driving a Conestoga wagon train west. We had to figure out what provisions to take, what we might encounter, how to get there."

JT cinched the draw cord on his daypack and shouldered it. "Ah, yeah, I remember that sort of thing."

"What strikes me now is that up to that point I'd never thought about going to a place that no one could tell you anything about." I looked across the tundra toward a cluster of low mountains and tried to imagine what was on the other side.

"You were into spaceships too, weren't you?" he said, remembering. "You went to space camp!" he blurted, trying to make fun of me. It'd been too long since I'd heard him laugh like that. I didn't want him to stop.

"Dude," I replied in mock smugness, sticking my nose in the air. "I won most valuable teen astronaut on my spaceship's mission."

JT and I walked toward a small rise, and I was lost in thoughts of exploration and discovery. I'll never go to outer space, but I could feel like an explorer on the frontier right there where I was. I knew I was not actually the first person to walk there, but it felt like it.

"Can you find where we are?" I asked JT, and he pointed to a spot on the map where two drainages came together. We spun around 360 degrees trying to decide which valley looked most enticing, which twist in the terrain would draw us in.

"Any idea what the walking is like in these drainages?" JT asked me.

"Who knows," I responded, wondering how far the drainage closest to us went. "It looks like bear country, though."

"Based on—?" He looked at me skeptically.

"Based on the fact that if I were a bear, I'd want to be walking up that drainage. Look how cute the creek is!"

He rolled his eyes, but I could tell that he too thought the little creek was pretty cool. "Okay," he said, nodding in that direction, "let's go."

We followed the tinkling creek as it wrapped into the mountains, until the gravel streambed got narrower and narrower and we had to climb up the banks to avoid getting our feet wet. This trip to the Arctic wasn't supposed to happen. We'd already taken the Last Trip Together before Parenthood. Throughout the summer I'd stayed on the drugs and we'd continued trying to get me pregnant. We'd crossed everything off the list that might hold us back from embracing our role as parents. We lost interest in the training and racing that had once occupied so much of our time. We spent more time caring for our home. I stopped thinking about the adult trips, the spontaneous outings with friends, and the quiet moments to myself that would be greatly reduced if we had a child. Instead I'd become interested in the new things we would experience as parents. I thought about family walks in the Chugach, discovering the world through the eyes of a young person, and feeling the strongest bond anyone can feel for another human. Yet it was as if we'd opened a new chapter only to find a blank page. We stared dumbfounded at the page and hoped for words that weren't there.

When August had rolled around, I'd needed a break from the weekly doctor's appointments. I needed a timeout from people asking how I was and feeling like I couldn't answer honestly. Joy's athletic restrictions only applied if I was pregnant, so after the August pregnancy test was negative, we'd booked a flight up north.

After a couple hours of walking, JT pointed up to our right. "Look at that." Neither of us could resist the carpet of tundra that appeared to roll right up to the sky. We followed the ramp uphill over pink bursts of moss campion and patches of bluebells to the top of a gentle ridge. At the top we sat back-to-back, breathing in the panorama and rummaging through our sack of food. We passed each other handfuls of nuts and dried bananas.

The landscape looked remarkably barren: scree-filled chutes dribbled off the sides of mountains, cold clouds hovered overhead, and gravel bars, white as bone, corralled the creek. From our perch, I was struck by how much land there was and how little water. How empty the gravel bar looked twisting below us through big mountains. The creek was mint and runny, and I could see right through the water to the cobbles on the bottom. I thought of the web of rivers in the Arctic as arteries, delivering the lifeblood of the land. Like a conveyer belt clanking over cobbles, the stream below rolled along over rocks and around knolls of land, making life here possible. Plant communities thrive along river corridors, and animals come to drink. We came here too, drawn to a gentle current that led us up valleys and down others, like the whisper of an old friend.

I felt that at any moment an animal might pass by. I scanned the wide-open space with binoculars, brimming with anticipation, the possibility of peering through a window into a world that exists during all the time we are not here to observe it. The land we walked over felt alive.

It practically pulsed with caribou hooves, thrummed with the energy of four hundred thousand migrating ungulates, the wolves and bears pursuing them, and the scavengers cleaning up all that's left behind.

The only trails were the ones made by caribou, blazed with bone and skulls, fur and hoof and hide, reminders that life swells and vacates twice a year as the Northwest Arctic Caribou Herd heads north to the coastal plain to calve and then south again for the winter. I hoped to see a wolf, but so far we'd only seen their paw prints polka-dotting the sandy river bar. So much went on here I didn't know about, so many aspects of nature my eyes never see.

"Think about Lower 48 wilderness," said JT out of the blue. "Trails up mountains. No bushwhacking, no river crossings. Roads to bail out on if you need help. Can you imagine sharing the wilderness with all those people?"

"Can you imagine sharing it with *anyone*?" I said. The second the words escaped my lips I regretted saying them. I felt compelled to add, "Except, of course, with our child," but I didn't. We hadn't talked about children since we'd been out here.

But then I had to say it. "I wonder how it's possible to feel such satisfaction in this place when I know there's something really big missing from our lives," I said.

JT sighed. "I know. Everything else feels right, but every day I think about having kids."

———

The next day we entertained ourselves by trying to suspend our bodies leaning forward into a strong wind. And then it started raining a cold and driving rain. Since it's impossible to predict what kind of weather these Arctic mountains might stir up, we continued on our route, business as usual. There was no sense waiting for a perfect day, because it might never come.

My hooded windbreaker flapped deafeningly against the side of my head. It was the kind of wind that made me dizzy. After a long day of walking in it, the sensation swirled in my head long after I got in the tent, in the middle of alders on a brushy gravel bar. My face felt chapped, my eyes gritty and red.

"I'm nervous about camping here, so close to all the bear trails," I said.

"I can't sleep in the howling wind," he insisted. The wind is why we stopped in the alders instead of up on the bench with better visibility.

"Well *I* can't sleep if I'm being munched by a bear," I said.

But he just looked at me like I was being overly dramatic. As we lay back in our sleeping bags I thought, *What if he's wrong? Should I have insisted we camp up higher?* Even in that sheltered spot, the wind was so loud we wouldn't hear a bear even if one was right outside our tent. But I didn't say anything. Too tired to argue, I accepted the decision and noticed something euphoric about releasing myself from worry and acknowledging that there was no longer anything I could do about it. I thought to myself, *Surrender*, and I ended up sleeping better than I thought I would.

A couple of days later we found ourselves sitting at camp with only one intention: looking around. Alaskans understand that when the perfect conditions present themselves, you express profound gratitude and overstate how incredulous you are. It is your duty and obligation to sit at camp and marvel at everything. We stopped hiking at noon so that we could pitch the tent and do this.

I tucked a lock of greasy hair behind my ear and felt the sun on my face. North of us, on an east–west trajectory, was the Continental Divide. This jumble of peaks is the last great wrinkle of the North American continent before the earth slopes down toward the Arctic Ocean. Inaccessible Ridge rose like a wall before us, and from my perspective it lives up to its name, but yesterday JT scrambled through the cliff bands to the top.

We napped beside the trickling creek. We took pictures of wildflowers and expansive green valleys fingering up toward big rocky peaks. We washed socks in the creek and hung them on the tent to dry. We cooked lentil stew and ate chocolate-covered almonds and Thai-spiced cashews. We regretted not having brought wine.

I shifted positions on the squishy ground beside our tent, where we reclined onto our backpacks and rubbed our pale toes across scratchy lichens and colorful flowers. It was quiet. I heard only a light breeze on my ear, the buzz of a bee on pink dwarf fireweed, and the occasional squawk of a gull. JT looked serene, which I thought had a lot to do with how he'd been spending his time while he waited for me to get pregnant.

A few months ago he'd asked, "What would you think about adopting a child?"

We had talked about adoption from time to time over the preceding couple of years, tossing it around as one option among many for building a family.

"I don't want to give up on having our own kid," he'd said, "but I'll understand if you want to stop trying."

"Thanks. I'm not ready to quit yet, but I appreciate you saying that. Either way, I think you're right—adoption could be an option."

"At least get the process started," he'd said, which had seemed reasonable to me, and so he'd begun to compile information.

JT is a doer. While I'd been learning to surrender, he must take action. The idea of adoption had given him a project, a way forward.

Considering our passion for travel and affinity for Latin American culture, we'd decided on international adoption. There were only a few Latin American countries open to adoption by US parents, and we learned that some won't adopt younger children to a couple approaching or surpassing the elderly age of forty. Some programs are so dysfunctional that we were warned to not even bother with them, and others can take more than five years to place a child. We'd settled on Honduras, a country we knew almost nothing about. We'd interviewed adoption agencies, signed a contract, checked a box beside *Honduras*, and sent the agency a hefty check. They'd sent us a pile of forms and instructions, and for the next few months we'd completed adoption paperwork, hoping that each document, each notarized signature, apostille, and letter of recommendation put us one step closer to having a family.

I'd heard JT diplomatically explain our choice to his conservative aging father in Georgia. "We feel that a multicultural family symbolizes diversity and acceptance," he'd said.

That's how we'd answered one of the questions on the adoption application, saying that international adoption to us epitomized a one-world concept imbued with enough respect to celebrate individual differences. JT and I both found it exciting to consider that our family would have ties to a variety of cultures, languages, and geographies.

Matt had traveled to Honduras a few years before and raved about the friendly, welcoming people, gorgeous coastlines and vibrant mountain communities. We had also learned that Honduras is one of the poorest and most corrupt countries in the world. As we had dived deeper into the adoption process and watched piles of paperwork increase exponentially, we'd watched Honduras's murder rate do the same. The United Nations declared Honduras the most violent country in the world, with a murder rate four times that of Mexico's. The Peace Corps deemed it too dangerous and pulled out all of their volunteers. The national police were reportedly corrupt at every level and the citizens besieged by poverty, violence, and drug trafficking. A child's future there seemed bleak to us.

"There's no shortage of kids in orphanages," Matt had told us. "There are kids who've lost their parents and many more whose families just can't take care of them."

I thought about the friends I'd made during my travels in Peru. I recalled how hard they worked and how much they suffered. How unfair their lives seemed to me. The reality was that no matter how hard they tried, there was little chance that their quality of life would improve. There was too much corruption, too great a suppression of darker-skinned people, too large a gap between the upper and lower classes. We could change that for a child. But it also felt complicated. Did our privileged status as white Americans give us the right to extract a child from his or her homeland, culture, and community? Who were we to swoop in and change a child's destiny? And then I thought, *With all the means and opportunity we have, who were we* not *to?*

It felt good to think that we'd be giving a child an opportunity that otherwise might not exist, but it wasn't an act of pure altruism. We felt like we needed a child as much as a child might need us.

"It's such a good thing you're doing," my mom had said. "That child will be so lucky."

"Yeah, I hope so," I'd replied. "But we'll be lucky too. Plus, there's a lot of loss that I think we need to acknowledge."

For a family, community, and country to be suffering so profoundly that they must give up their *children*, things have to be absolutely desperate.

"This is a pretty tough thing for everyone involved," I'd heard JT tell his dad over the phone. "We're not expecting to be showered in gratitude." Our adoption agency representative had told us to expect a variety of reactions when we traveled to Honduras to meet the child. She'd said that some people might be glad that we were providing a better life for one of their own but that others might resent us for what might seem like stealing their children.

The more we'd learned about adoption, the more we'd realized that there is profound pain for everyone involved: our own pain of struggling to start a family, that of the suffering Honduran mother who gives up her baby, and the heartache of the child whose birth family, community, and country were not able to keep him or her.

In the end, we were hoping that everyone would benefit more than they would suffer. We hoped that we would ultimately be able to bring a child into our family, that the birth family would be assured that their child would be cared for and loved. We hoped to offer a different pairing so that all of us—the child, JT, and I—might start down a new path and see where it led.

———

JT and I had recently completed the home study and put the finishing touches on our dossier. We'd learned a few things in the process. International adoption requires a *lot* of paperwork. It involves what could be perceived as unnecessary probing by complete strangers into the most personal aspects of prospective adoptive parents' lives, more money than I care to mention, and complete uncertainty.

Our parents had asked what kind of child we expected to get.

"A Honduran one."

The truth was that we had requested a healthy child of either gender under the age of three, but who knows what type of child we'd be matched with.

Our parents had asked how long the process would take.

"No idea."

They'd asked where we were in the process.

"Requirements seem to change weekly."

They'd wanted to know when we'd travel to Honduras and how long we'd have to stay.

"No idea where we'll be going. No idea when or for how long. Not sure how much advance notice we'll be given."

Did we know the country was in turmoil?

"We're sure it's safe where we'll be going," we'd lied.

———————

"It's a strange thing to think about," I told JT as we lounged among the sun-drenched forget-me-nots, watching the summer day unfold in the Arctic. "That we could have all this and still have so much uncertainty in our lives."

Our lives might drastically change at any moment. I might be able to have a biological baby. Our adoption agency might call with good news—or might tell us that Honduras, like several neighboring countries, had closed its doors to international adoption.

"You love mystery out here," JT said.

I did, and JT and I often had remarked on it. I found value in that uncomfortable feeling of vulnerability in the wilderness because it forced me to show up in each moment as my most authentic self. "But the mystery of this backcountry trip lasts only as long as the trip," I said. "The uncertainty of life in general—"

JT didn't reply. He looked at peace sprawled in the sunshine, but I suspected the contentment would not last long after we got home. JT would pine for another project. The close of the year would remind him that he was that much older and still not a father. Winter would descend and cast its dark shadow. We had sent a cosmic request to the universe asking for children, and we had no indication of how the universe might respond. Closing my eyes, I imagined that the months ahead would be like exploring this tundra valley with JT, planning our route as we went. Not knowing, not having it all figured out ahead of time in the backcountry, that's when I find that my personal edge, my frontier, is right before my eyes. Could it be the same at home?

But my eyes flew open, and the mystery I had cherished was gone like the summer breeze across the tundra.

WILD GRACE

Half a year later I was in the bathroom with a drugstore pregnancy detection kit. I held my breath as I waited for a plus or minus sign to appear. I squinted and braced for the news that, despite trying again, I was still not pregnant. When the stick showed a plus sign, I got a little surge as if I'd won the lottery, but then I sobered quickly and thought *here we go again.* Could I handle it?

When I told JT he hugged me and looked hopeful, but we didn't say much.

Every day I looked at the toilet paper for signs of blood. I didn't answer the phone. I postponed dinner invitations. I sat in my room and meditated on the sturdy mountain ridges above our house. I watched spring slip gracefully into summer, and I gazed at eagles circling in the drafts over my backyard. I found peace in the tiny creek, the trembling stalks of purple monk's hood, and sunlight on evening hills.

When I was into the third month, farther than the preceding pregnancies, I cradled my belly and smiled at JT.

"I don't want to jinx it," he said softly, "but when is the due date?"

"December," I smiled. "A winter baby."

"I wonder if it's a boy or a girl," he said, putting his hand on my belly. "We don't have to wait much longer to find out."

We smiled more and started joking again.

That was before the night JT and I went out to dinner and laughed so hard. It was before I went to the bathroom when we got home and before I noticed a tinge of pink on the toilet paper. It was before I texted Joy, and it was before the labs were done. It was before the ultrasound, before they searched for that little fluttering heart and couldn't find one. It was before I sat in Joy's office trying to be strong and accept the facts, before she told me that she knew how hard this was because she too had lost three before she had her twins. It was before she wrapped her arms around me in her office and I started to sob.

———

I've heard grace defined as God's gift of infinite love to humankind. I sometimes wonder if wilderness isn't also God's gift of infinite love and whether that might explain my desire to be in wild places, that I yearn for nature in order to tap into grace. Often I do it modestly, dipping a timid finger into the current of wildness and stepping back to see if that one touch is all it might take to transform me.

Grace, I think, can also act as a mirror that reflects my highest self. I imagine a moment when my body is moving in a way that feels like the perfect union of motion, form, and flow. When I achieve this, even for a moment, I feel possessed by a power higher than myself, as if whatever activity I'm doing is dancing and I am the most perfect expression of that dance.

I've seen grace. When I watch JT climbing a cliff, I know without a doubt that he'll make it to the top, although he's not assisted by ropes or climbing gear. He reaches up with his right arm, turns sideways to get the longest reach, and then effortlessly pulls himself up as if humans, like the mountain goats on the adjacent slope, were meant to walk vertical paths instead of horizontal ones. He places his toe on a speck of slanted rock that miraculously supports his weight. His hand automatically finds a hold, as if his arm is an extension of the rock ledge. I look at the same pitch and am terrified. JT looks built for this, his lanky limbs reaching into impossible places, the strength of his core levitating upward. I think to myself that he was meant to be right there, right now, doing just this, tiptoeing up a cliff. And perhaps this is grace too.

Often I see grace in nature. About a week after the third pregnancy loss, I wandered through a field of lupines in the valley near our house. The green leaves of the lupines looked like upside down umbrellas, and each leaf cradled pearls of water from the night's dew. The fronds curled up just enough so that each droplet was perfectly balanced, as if tenderly cupped in the palm of a hand. A breeze shivered the plants, and the little pearls trembled, but unless I kicked them while hiking, each drop of water remained cupped.

I wandered out one day to explore the freshness of spring, when the dusty browns of wilted winter were beginning to turn rich, green, and promising. Spring happens quickly in Alaska, usually over the course of a couple days. Everything pushes up at once and rushes to grow in the almost round-the-clock sunlight. I walked among brand-new leaves and shoots and noticed how pure they looked, how untouched they were by the bugs, disease, and weather that would come later in summer.

When I looked up from the field of lupines, something brown caught my eye. In a second it registered as a moose standing in the meadow up ahead. Off to the side I saw another smudge of brown, her calf. I quietly moved toward them to get a better view, but she must have been suspicious of me because she started walking away. When I think of graceful creatures, moose aren't the first that come to mind, but as I watched the large cow move her mass through brambles and brush and over jumbles of fallen trees, I couldn't help but feel she did so with a steady and persistent grace.

As I watched her walk, though, I noticed that her coat was frayed and mangy after the long winter. There was beauty in her movement but not in her physical appearance. Clumps of coarse gray-brown fur hung off her body. Scars along her back and ribs exposed leathery skin. She was an island of imperfection in a sea of flawlessness. Her calf, probably only a few days old, had a glossy brown coat—soft, supple, and unblemished. I watched the two of them wade through the vibrant green leaves of spring. They paused, looked around, and resumed nibbling juicy shoots.

As I walked through the valley with the moose, I thought about what someone had said to me the day before. She'd asked the question I'd been dreading, and she'd said it so matter-of-factly that she must have never known that kind of pain.

"So," she'd probed. "Do you and JT have kids?"

Answering that question had become difficult, but I'd managed this time with a firm but pleasant, "No, we don't," meant to end the conversation. But she'd persisted.

"Don't you want a little bundle to take with you on all the trips you do? You guys should have kids." As if you can walk into a store and pick one up.

I'd excused myself, turned around, taken a deep breath, and cried as I walked away. I'd felt like the tattered moose. I yearned for graceful acceptance, but I couldn't find it. We'd been trying for more than eighteen months to have a child: a year and a half anxiously sitting in doctors' waiting rooms, lining up containers of prescription drugs, and watching patiently as the phlebotomist drew vial after vial of blood for innumerable tests. A year and a half of living with a private, quiet pain. Each time I'd gotten pregnant, my hope of having a child had soon crumbled. Each time, I'd dropped the toilet paper into the bowl as if it were alive and flushed it down quickly as if trying to get rid of a spider that might crawl back out.

I couldn't look at pregnant women or watch children without feeling sad. I felt myself forcing a smile for only as long as it was necessary. At night I stared at the ceiling and wondered who those babies might have grown up to be. I didn't want to leave the house. I didn't want to see friends, because I knew I couldn't fake being happy. And I didn't want to drag my most beloved friends into a well of despair. When someone asked me how I was doing and what I'd been up to, I couldn't bring myself to say, "Fine, just the same old thing; doing fine, thanks." Which is why I wanted to stay in my cave.

Alone there I was consumed by my desire to be a mother. I shed angry tears when I thought that having a child should come as part of the package of being human. It seems so fundamental to our society and our biology.

One night I broke down crying.

"What's going on?" asked JT softly.

I covered my head with a pillow and felt ill in every cell of my body.

"What's wrong with me?" I blurted. "I can't do this most basic thing that everyone else can do." Heroin addicts can do this. Sixteen-year-old high school dropouts can do this. Those gruff women who curse at their kids as they drag them by their upper arms through the aisles at Walmart can have kids. Not me.

"Honey," JT said tentatively. "There's nothing wrong with you." He gently rubbed my back as I cried.

At first I vowed to be supportive of my friends who were having babies (they all seemed to be), and I did my best to smile at baby showers. At first I stuck to it and was genuinely happy about their happiness, but this came to remind me what I didn't have. I no longer went to baby showers. It was just too hard to be around that sort of joy. I was at the bottom of the pond. It was murky down there, but I wasn't interested in coming up.

I lay at the bottom for a long time, long enough for nothing to matter anymore. Weeks passed, and then for no particular reason I stopped fighting. I stopped wanting. And I thought, *When you hit bottom, is that some form of grace too?* Maybe acceptance can be a type of grace. Maybe forgiveness can. I began a new ritual: every night I listed a few things for which I felt grateful. This ritual helped me to realize that there wasn't room to hold on to that much pain when there were things to be grateful for. Like another chance.

A few months later we conceived a fourth time. I found out on a cold January morning. This time I was not sure if the *yes* on the stick was something to celebrate or dread. I stared out the window into the darkness.

The losses hadn't left me. Probably they never would. But by this time they sat quietly beside me instead of yanking me down. That night I was making my gratitude list, and for some reason the memory popped into my head of walking through the valley with the moose. I felt grateful for her lovely gait and tattered coat, the promise of grace prevailing. I felt grateful for her reminder that not one of us remains whole, intact, or unblemished. This is what unites us: the certainty of scars and tattered pelts.

And the moments of grace when we carry on despite them.

AVERY

Some people might say it was risky to fly to a remote destination in Lake Clark National Park when I was six months pregnant. Particularly since it was my fourth pregnancy and—because of the three prior losses, a blood-clotting disorder, and the fact that I was nearing forty—considered high-risk. *I am only going for a few days,* I told myself. I wasn't going to do anything strenuous—just spend a couple of nights at a lake in the wilderness. I'd be camping less than a half mile from where the floatplane would drop me off.

I wanted to go because I wanted to feel normal. For the first time in half a year I would be more than an hour from a hospital. After six months of restricted activity, daily pill-popping to safeguard the pregnancy, a nightly injection of a blood thinner to prevent my body from attacking the fetus, and a constant barrage of tests, and all of this preceded by two difficult years on and off the pregnancy roller coaster, I wanted to do one thing I normally do in the summer, which is to get into the Alaska backcountry. To touch the wilderness one last time before, I hoped, my life would change forever.

So despite my precarious situation, I flew on a tiny plane, hemmed in between stacked luggage and cases of Dr. Pepper, over a bumpy Lake Clark Pass toward Port Alsworth. Joy would not have approved, which is why I hadn't told her. In the sunlight, a waterfall, like a cascade of stars, spilled from a hanging glacier. There was more snow than I expected, white snow that covered the ash from the last Mount Redoubt eruption. Bergschrunds creased the upper couloirs, and snowball avalanches streaked down chutes, smearing the gullies gray with tilled rocks. The North Fork came into view, and I thought about the trip JT and I did over there, how hard it had been to find our way off that glacier, and then how lovely it was packrafting back to Lake Clark. I knew the secrets beyond those turning valley walls, how the river comes out of that glacier and the glacier comes out of the jumble of mountains. It seemed like forever ago. When I had been leading a different life.

I cradled my belly with my left hand and, with the other, held the seat belt away from the bulge. I felt for her kicks, which had been coming frequently. Especially in the evenings, JT and I had been lying in bed and watching my belly move, trying to guess if it was a foot or a hand or a butt cheek thrusting out. It had been an undecipherable Morse code of kicks and punches, and we'd been smiling and clinging to each one.

In the quiet moments, I'd welled up with tears thinking how much I loved her already. It was difficult to comprehend my growing capacity for love and how I would possibly manage such emotion when she was out of the womb and I could actually hold and kiss her.

During other times fear and worry had possessed my thoughts. I'd had crazy dreams, vivid and often of people I know. Sometimes they had died tragic deaths, and I'd transitioned in and out of sleep fighting to quash the nightmares. I couldn't seem to stop myself from daydreaming about losing the baby. I'd told JT that I'd been worrying incessantly, especially when he'd been out of town on summer fishing trips.

"Are you going to be one of those parents who bubble-wraps their kid every time they leave the house?" he'd joked.

"I hope not," I'd replied honestly, "but I'm not sure."

I'd never thought I'd be paranoid that the baby wasn't moving enough or that she was moving too much or that the latest discomfort meant there was something wrong. But I'd also never thought that I'd be on my fourth pregnancy and still not have a child. Maybe it's a side effect of being haunted by loss.

———

When the floatplane landed at the lake and I stepped onto the gravel beach, it felt cold for June. The air was damp, and chunks of ice bobbed in the lake. All of the mountains were streaked with snow.

Dark clouds gathered overhead, and I quickly pitched my tent in a lumpy patch of Labrador tea and moss just a few feet from the thin gravel shore. A cold wind flapped the nylon wall and unleashed a driving rain as I pawed through the door and pushed my belongings to the far end.

Later in the afternoon I was still nestled there on the lakeshore, and it was raining hard. The tent door opened toward the lake, and I sat at the threshold, mesmerized by the expanse of water before me. It was like looking straight into a wet, dripping mouth. My baby kicked hard as I watched rain spatter the surface of the lake. I was glad I'd brought an old plastic yogurt container to pee in so that I didn't have to go out in the cold rain every hour when the weight of the growing baby created an unpleasant urge to pee.

I was also glad I'd brought a down comforter, since my belly didn't fit into a sleeping bag. Feeling decadent but deserving, I'd also brought a body pillow to support my legs and belly at night. The pillow and comforter felt damp from the rain, but it still felt luxurious to have such comforts so far from civilization.

My mom would be glad that I brought the comforter. In the 1970s she bought an eight-person canvas monstrosity with clunky metal poles and encouraged us to have camping parties in our backyard. She and Dad made sure we had heaps of blocky cotton sleeping bags and pillows, and still we city kids ran back to the house when we were the slightest bit cold or scared or hungry. I remembered the smell of canvas, green grass underfoot, freshly cut blades sticking to my heels and between my toes, and, waiting for us inside, Mom's carved-out watermelon basket filled with balls of watermelon, cantaloupe, and honeydew melon. Would I be that kind of mom?

The temperature was just above freezing, and I wrapped the comforter around my shoulders. I filled my lungs with cool, cleansing air and closed my eyes for a moment to revel in the smells and sounds of being back in the wilderness. Clouds rose up and sank down the sides of snow-streaked mountains as if they were on an invisible elevator.

As cold as it was, I still needed to give myself an injection of Lovenox, the blood thinner that I'd been injecting into my abdomen every night. It was a dreaded ritual. The fluid burned as it went in and felt like acid pooling beneath my skin. Every night I screamed until the burning subsided. JT had administered the injection at home, but out here I would have to do it myself. One thing was for sure: ice eased the pain. And there was a patch of ice just down to the left of my tent, clinging to cobbles and encrusting about twenty feet of shoreline, winter's last relic. It was a good thing, that ice patch.

Although I didn't want to leave the warmth of the tent, I knew I had to get it over with. I dragged my big belly up, put my raincoat on, stepped outside, and waddled down to the ice patch with a plastic bag. The ice was littered with dirt and leaves, which I brushed aside with my bare hand. I chipped off a hunk of ice and scooped it into the bag. Then I rolled up layers of shirts and jackets and grimaced as I put the ice on my stomach. After a couple of minutes I wiped an alcohol pad across my belly, tore open a syringe, pinched some belly fat with my wet, dirt-stained fingers, took a deep breath, and injected the needle. I slowly pushed the plunger despite the urge to yank it out. It seared as usual, and I pulled my cold hand up into the cuff of my down jacket as I pressed the ice against my stomach, waiting for the sting to dull.

The rain let up. Stillness and quiet hung heavily over the water like a wet cloud. A goldeneye perched on the top of a spruce outside my tent. A loon threw a long call from across the lake, from somewhere in the mist. Beads of water dripped off my tent as I looked through the door at wisps of clouds opening and closing like a phantom curtain, revealing and concealing different patches of lake and mountain.

The lake was clear. I could see every rock cobbling the bottom and only an occasional ripple marking the water's skin. I was overcome by a quiet peace, and I thought, *This is where we come to lick our wounds.* I wanted to stay up all night watching because I knew I'd be there for such a short time. Two nights would not feel like nearly enough. But it was all the time I had.

When the plane came to pick me up, I touched my belly and whispered, "I hope you get to see this place."

Shortly after I returned home, I woke up just like I did every morning and started to get ready for work. But this morning, so unexpectedly, there was blood. I called Joy.

"It might be nothing," she said. "But let's take a look. The ultrasound clinic opens at nine. Start driving, and I'll let them know you're coming."

JT was out of town and out of cell range. Fighting back tears, I got in the car and thought, *No. Not after six months. Not after all we've been through.*

I drove to the clinic with one hand on the steering wheel and one hand on my stomach, trying to feel my baby move. I moved my fingers across the taut skin and poked at various bulges, but there was no response. How dare JT leave me alone with this precarious baby and all the nos piled up around me, caging me in: no exercise, no yoga, no sex, no caffeine, no alcohol, no dancing, no backcountry trips. I didn't care that he had bought a crib and a box of children's books, done all the home-maintenance chores, and set up the nursery. He was not there then when I needed him.

As I sat in the waiting room staring at cheery magazine covers, a feeling of hopelessness came over me. A couple entered and signed in at the reception desk. The young man rested his hand on his partner's lower back, and I saw her relax. I stiffened and hardened my expression. I turned all my weepy emotion to stone.

The ultrasound technician lubed my belly and placed the wand on my abdomen. My face was blank. I was numb. I lay back in the dark room and stared at the glowing monitor on the wall. She rubbed the wand back and forth across my abdomen and I waited for her to shatter my world.

"There's baby's heart," she said finally. I held my breath and braced for the worst.

"It's beating," she said.

I released the breath I'd been holding.

She measured the heart rate. "One hundred thirty. Baby's doing fine."

My eyes filled with tears. "Okay," I said quietly through quivering lips.

After a thorough examination, she sent me home to rest, just in case. But my little girl was okay. At least for the moment, she was fine. *Just a few more months*, I thought. *You just have to make it until October.*

———————

It was October 6, and Tony and Becky were getting married. JT drove into the parking lot at Arctic Valley, and we saw our friends filing into the ski lodge. Matt pulled in next to us, and we stepped out of our vehicles. Matt stared at my belly, which was not enormous like it was when we had dinner last week. His mouth contorted. He stuttered and didn't know what to say. He didn't know what had happened.

JT set him at ease. "Matt," he said, putting an arm around his shoulders. "We'd like you to meet our daughter, Avery."

I opened the back door so he could see the tiny five-pound infant nestled in blankets asleep in the car seat. "She's two days old. She had to bust out of the hospital, but there was no way she was going to miss Tony and Bec getting married."

Matt gave me a hug. "How did the delivery go?"

I picked up Avery and held her to my chest. "It still feels kind of surreal and miraculous. As for childbirth, there's no pain quite like it. I can't even compare it to suffering in the wilderness."

Matt grimaced. "No drugs?"

"No," I said proudly, "but I understand now why people use them."

Once inside, I felt like we'd arrived at a family reunion. Tony and Becky rushed over to peek at Avery's sleeping face. Becky wrapped her arm around me and whispered to my chest, "You're in for a great life, little girl."

In December there was only an inch of snow in Threebowls. I put on an oversized jacket, grabbed my trekking poles, and headed up the mountain. I carefully picked my way through the willows and slowly climbed up toward the ridge. Although the winter sun would only be up for a short time, the day was clear. It had been a long time since I'd been up there.

As I hiked, the crunch of snow became a mantra, and I stared at the ground to make sure I didn't slip on the snow. After an hour I triumphantly stood on top of the ridge.

I unzipped the top of my oversized jacket and peered down at my chest. My little girl, just two months old, was wrapped snugly against me. Her eyes were closed, and she squeaked a little as she nuzzled into my fleece jacket. I looked across the Chugach peaks.

"Hey, little Avery," I whispered to her, "Do you see how beautiful the world is?"

I pulled her hat down over her ear and held her tiny hand. "We're so glad you chose us," I said. "I hope you like where you landed."

I slowly spun around and pointed out Denali, the tallest mountain in North America; the slow, meandering Eagle River across the frosty valley floor; and the great swatch of swirling ice and water in Knik Arm. The early afternoon sunset made everything glow pink.

"This is your home, Love," I told her.

On the way down the mountain I reflected on what wild places meant to me now. The birth of my daughter, against all odds, had given me another reason to feel grateful for wild places. It is in the wilderness that I have gained clarity in the sea of my own conflicting thoughts and emotions around motherhood. Wilderness has taught me perseverance, challenged me to test my edges, calmed and nurtured me in my darkest moments. I wanted Avery to have the chance to find peace, joy, and inspiration in wild places, just as I have.

I cradled her little head and hugged her into me. "Alaska is a very special place," I whispered, as if telling her a secret. "It's a place where miracles happen."

That evening JT and I sat with my parents in our living room and talked about raising a child in Alaska.

"With these mountains in her backyard," said Mom, "she'll be skiing before you know it."

"I remember my friend telling me that his kids, after a long winter, were afraid of the sun," I said, and we all laughed.

"Alaska kids sure don't grow up the way we did on fresh-cut lawns, with family trips to see musicals in New York City," said JT.

"Or with beach vacations to the Jersey Shore," added Dad.

"How old does she have to be before you teach her what to do if she sees a bear?" wondered Mom.

Part of me wanted to continue the traditions that my parents created for my brother and me. The other part of me was excited to raise a child in such a unique place. Here kids live in a snow-covered world most of the year. They are bundled in layers of clothes. They eat salmon the way I ate peanut butter sandwiches. Their chores might include feeding a dog team. They have moose and wolverines in their backyards.

We hoped we could offer Avery, and, if our Honduran adoption goes through, her future brother or sister, a unique way of ordering the world: a creative community of friends who feel like family, a healthy outdoor lifestyle, a home surrounded by natural beauty—surely these things are good for the soul. That and a whole lot of love are all we can promise to provide, and we hope it's enough.

Later in the evening, Mom got up and started scrubbing the corners of our kitchen floor and washing all the cabinets, two things that had not happened in more than a decade here. She offered to change Avery's dirty diaper and asked if there was anything else she could do. When I did my nighttime gratitude ritual, I was grateful for my parents and wished they were staying more than a month.

At 4:00 a.m. Dad was waiting for me in the rocking chair like he did every morning during that month. Exhausted from another sleepless night nursing, I carefully walked downstairs, deposited Avery onto his lap, and returned to bed to try to get a couple hours of sleep.

"Avery Lee," I heard him say over and over to the little girl named in his honor.

At 7:00 a.m. I came back down and he was still holding her.

"My god, Dad. You've been holding her the whole time? You know you can put her on the couch."

He looked upon the sleeping infant in his arms, his one and only grandchild.

Dad looked up at me with heavy-lidded eyes. "I didn't want to wake her up," he said softly.

I carried Avery back upstairs to nurse her. Sitting on my bed, I looked out my bedroom window into the cold winter darkness. The silhouetted ridge where we stood yesterday afternoon was backlit by moonlight and starlight. Little Avery cooed as she nursed. I inhaled deeply and gazed through the glass. Stars swirled across the sky like glitter tossed to the wind, like fleeting moments of hope and joy.

ACKNOWLEDGMENTS

I'm indebted to many for helping me bring this book to life.

Above all, I'm deeply grateful for my family for the greatest gift: unconditional support and love. Mom and Dad, thank you for allowing me to choose my own path, even when you could see it would lead to a steep-walled ravine choked with devil's club.

Scott and Nathalie, you continually teach me what generosity looks like. Thank you for letting me invade your home for weeks at a time to work on early versions of these chapters and for supplying me with enough chocolate and oolong tea to write ten books.

Thank you, Margery Kerr, for being a reliable anchor during each passing storm.

Holly, my soul sister, thank you for inspiring me to go west and for encouraging me to write, always.

Matt Rafferty, Corrina Batten, Becky King, Tony Perelli, Sharon Flowers, and James Englehart, your comments and insights greatly improved the work.

Two of my heroes, Art Davidson and Kim Heacox, your words of encouragement have meant more than you'll know.

Thank you to Masie Cochran and Tricia Dowcett-Battencourt, whose edits on early drafts made me believe this project was possible, and to Kirsten Colten at the Friendly Red Pen. I could not have produced this book without your suggestions.

For believing in me and my story, thank you to Kate Rogers and Mountaineers Books. It was a pleasure to work with you.

Any errors or faults of this book are my own.

To all of my National Park Service colleagues who work to keep Alaska's parks wild, thank you for fighting for what matters most and for ensuring America's best idea lives on. For your inspiration and guidance, a heartfelt thank you to Judy Alderson, Joe Van Horn, Roger Kaye, Page Spencer, Mike Tranel, Steve Carwile, Dick Anderson, Jeff Yanuchi, Jeanne Schaaf, Tim Devine, Peter Landres, Peter Christian, and Dan Stevenson.

It takes a community to make a home, and I'm grateful for the Katimmavik community, which early on provided a way for me to find my people. To my Alaska family who have shared hearts, stories, salmon, tents, tears, belly laughs, mediocre ukulele playing, bottomless moose crocks, living room floors, plenty of unreasonable trip ideas, and most of the best moments of my life—the mountains are the reason I came, but you are the reason I stayed.

Thank you, Joy Zimmerman-Golden, for making Avery possible.

Finally, thank you to my husband, JT, who never asked for some of the most personal details of his life to become part of a book but who supported me anyway.

ABOUT THE AUTHOR

Adrienne Lindholm lives in Eagle River, Alaska, where she oversees the Wilderness Stewardship Program for the national parks in Alaska. Since 2000 she has worked for the National Park Service as a backcountry ranger, park planner, compliance officer, and natural resource manager. She is also a mother, speaker, and writer.

In addition to a memoir about thru-hiking the Appalachian Trail, she's the author of several backpacking guidebooks, and her essays and articles have appeared in a variety of magazines and literary journals. She is inspired by wild unhindered places, the flash of wonder in her daughter's eyes, and passionate friends and strangers who work to create a more compassionate and just world. For more information about Adrienne and her work, visit adriennelindholm.com.

MOUNTAINEERS BOOKS is a leading publisher of mountaineering literature and guides—including our flagship title, *Mountaineering: The Freedom of the Hills*—as well as adventure narratives, natural history, and general outdoor recreation. Through our two imprints, Skipstone and Braided River, we also publish titles on sustainability and conservation. We are committed to supporting the environmental and educational goals of our organization by providing expert information on human-powered adventure, sustainable practices at home and on the trail, and preservation of wilderness.

The Mountaineers, founded in 1906, is a 501(c)(3) nonprofit outdoor activity and conservation organization whose mission is "to explore, study, preserve, and enjoy the natural beauty of the outdoors." One of the largest such organizations in the United States, it sponsors classes and year-round outdoor activities throughout the Pacific Northwest, including climbing, hiking, backcountry skiing, snowshoeing, bicycling, camping, paddling, and more. The Mountaineers also supports its mission through its publishing division, Mountaineers Books, and promotes environmental education and citizen engagement. For more information, visit The Mountaineers Program Center, 7700 Sand Point Way NE, Seattle, WA 98115-3996; phone 206-521-6001; www.mountaineers.org; or email info@mountaineers.org.

Our publications are made possible through the generosity of donors and through sales of more than 800 titles on outdoor recreation, sustainable lifestyle, and conservation. To donate, purchase books, or learn more, visit us online:

MOUNTAINEERS BOOKS
1001 SW Klickitat Way, Suite 201• Seattle, WA 98134
800-553-4453 • mbooks@mountaineersbooks.org • www.mountaineersbooks.org

OTHER TITLES YOU MIGHT ENJOY FROM MOUNTAINEERS BOOKS

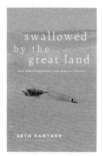

Swallowed by the Great Land:
And Other Dispatches from Alaska's Frontier
Seth Kantner
More than 50 slice-of-life essays and stories that explore
Kantner's life on the remote northwest coast of Alaska

Found:
A Life in Mountain Rescue
Bree Loewen
A search-and-rescue volunteer describes
intense recoveries, vivid wilderness
landscapes, and the warmth she discovers
in motherhood, community, and purpose

Forget Me Not:
A Memoir
Jennifer Lowe-Anker
An adventurous and insightful memoir about
the often complicated, yet ultimately
transformative, power of love

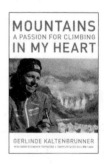

Mountains in My Heart:
A Passion for Climbing
Gerlinde Kaltenbrunner
The story of the first woman to climb
the world's fourteen 8000-meter
peaks without supplemental
oxygen or high-altitude porters

Minus 148°:
First Winter Ascent of Mount McKinley
Art Davidson
A gripping survival story of the team of eight men who
attempted the first winter ascent of Denali

www.mountaineersbooks.org